Praise for *Saving Aziz*

"From my depths of sadness and frustration about the war in Afghanistan, I saw the best of the American people as they gave their time, resources, and some, like Chad, risked it all to do the right thing and help our allies that sacrificed so much to assist us in our time of need. This is the story of why America remains the beacon of hope for the world."

—SECRETARY CHRISTOPHER MILLER, FORMER US SECRETARY OF
DEFENSE AND US ARMY SPECIAL FORCES COLONEL (RET.)

"More than a memoir, it is ultimately a story of purpose and redemption rooted in Chad's tenacious loyalty. It will leave you disappointed in America's leadership but proud to be an American. By book's end you will walk away with another, somewhat unexpected, feeling—hope."

—JACK CARR, US NAVY SEAL SNIPER (RET.), HOST OF THE *DANGER CLOSE* PODCAST,
AND #1 *NEW YORK TIMES* BESTSELLING AUTHOR OF THE TERMINAL LIST SERIES

"Marine veteran Chad Robichaux attempts an operation to save his Afghan interpreter, Aziz, and it turns into a mission that saves an astonishing 17,000 lives. This is a story you'll want to share."

—ERIC METAXAS, #1 *NEW YORK TIMES* BESTSELLING AUTHOR
AND HOST OF THE *ERIC METAXAS RADIO SHOW*

"Talk is cheap, and when thousands of men, women, and children were left behind in Afghanistan, it was time for some true warriors to take action. This gripping book tells their incredible story."

—JOCKO WILLINK, US NAVY SEAL (RET.), *NEW YORK TIMES* BESTSELLING
AUTHOR OF *EXTREME OWNERSHIP*, AND HOST OF THE *JOCKO PODCAST*

"*Saving Aziz* is the story of two warriors from different cultures brought together by war and a brotherhood forged through years of battling shoulder to shoulder for the cause of freedom. An absolute must-read."

—TIM KENNEDY, *NEW YORK TIMES* BESTSELLING AUTHOR OF *SCARS AND
STRIPES*, US ARMY SPECIAL FORCES SNIPER, UFC FIGHTER, FOUNDER
OF SHEEP DOG RESPONSE, AND COFOUNDER OF SAVE OUR ALLIES

"This incredible book details the courageous rescue of Aziz and his family—as well as seventeen thousand other Afgans, US, and allied citizens who were left behind.

This saga of brotherhood, loyalty, and raw courage will make you proud to be an American."

—GENERAL JAMES T. CONWAY, US MARINE CORPS (RET.),
THIRTY-FOURTH COMMANDANT OF THE US MARINE CORPS

"Chad Robichaux is one of the most honorable men I know, he is a perfect example of what a Marine truly is. His book, *Saving Aziz*, gives you firsthand insight on the man he is and why we should all aspire to be more like him."

—SERGEANT MAJOR MIKE GLOVER, US ARMY SPECIAL FORCES
SNIPER (RET.) AND FOUNDER AND CEO OF FIELDCRAFT SURVIVAL

"*Saving Aziz* is the spellbinding, must-read story of how a former Marine and member of SEAL Team Six acted on his desire to rescue his Afghan interpreter and saved seventeen thousand others in the process. Chad's faith, commitment to serve, and ability to assemble a team and take quick action made a huge difference. I highly recommend it."

—GREG BRENNEMAN, FORMER CEO OF CONTINENTAL AIRLINES,
BURGER KING, AND QUIZNOS; CHAIRMAN OF HOME DEPOT; AND
CURRENT EXECUTIVE CHAIRMAN OF CCMP CAPITAL

"Chad Robichaux is a national hero whose courage has saved lives and set an example of unselfish patriotism. I am proud to know Chad and am thankful he wrote this book so we can all know a real-life American hero."

—CONGRESSWOMAN VICKY HARTZLER, MISSOURI

"I am grateful for godly patriots like Chad. I commend him for his desire to honor the service that our Afghan brothers and sisters showed to the cause of freedom by helping them escape the ravages of the Taliban, including his friend, Aziz."

—PHIL ROBERTSON, FOUNDER OF DUCK COMMANDER, STAR OF
DUCK DYNASTY, AND *NEW YORK TIMES* BESTSELLING AUTHOR

"An amazing story of brotherhood, loyalty, sacrifice, service, and obedience to God. God uses Chad to save his brother-in-arms—and then to save thousands more. A must read. A true blessing."

—WAYNE KYLE, FATHER OF "AMERICAN SNIPER" CHRIS KYLE
AND PRESIDENT OF THE AMERICAN VALOR FOUNDATION

"*Saving Aziz* is a must-read for those who are longing to know if human goodness and sacrificial love still exist in our world today. One of the best command decisions I made in my humbling thirty-seven-year career in the Marine Corps was to favorably endorse the package that loaned one of our very best Recon Marine Sergeants to the Joint Special Operations community in 2003. I'm honored to have served with Chad, to continue to support him, and to know him as a great American and friend."

—MAJOR GENERAL JAMES HARTSELL, US MARINE CORPS (RET.) AND DIVISION COMMANDER AND EXECUTIVE DIRECTOR OF THE FLORIDA DEPARTMENT OF VETERANS' AFFAIRS

"*Saving Aziz* is a must-read for every American patriot, illustrating Chad Robichaux's bravery, compassion, and loyalty to allies and comrades-in-arms. God bless Chad and all the other great American warriors and humanitarians who have done so much for so many."

—LOU DOBBS, POLITICAL COMMENTATOR AND HOST OF *THE GREAT AMERICA SHOW*

"Chad tells the fascinating story of rescuing his friend and Afghani translator, Aziz, from the grasp of the Taliban. This book is the best account of the chaos of the evacuation of Afghanistan that I have read and also a great story of the warrior ethos."

—LIEUTENANT GENERAL "JERRY" BOYKIN, US ARMY SPECIAL FORCES (RET.), FOUNDING MEMBER OF THE US ARMY DELTA FORCE, US DEPUTY UNDERSECRETARY OF DEFENSE FOR INTELLIGENCE UNDER PRESIDENT GEORGE W. BUSH, EXECUTIVE VICE PRESIDENT OF THE FAMILY RESEARCH COUNCIL, AND AUTHOR

"*Saving Aziz* is the harrowing story of two men, separated by distance, culture, and religion who, drawing upon a bond forged in war, are each willing to lay down his life for the other."

—JIM SHANNON, CEO OF E3 PARTNERS MINISTRY AND I AM SECOND

"I implore you to read this impeccable exploit of how those who live by the creed 'Leave no one behind' will stand up to their own government and lead with honor."

—LIEUTENANT COLONEL ALLEN B. WEST, US ARMY (RET.), MEMBER OF THE 112TH US CONGRESS, AND FORMER CHAIRMAN OF THE REPUBLICAN PARTY OF TEXAS

"Saving Aziz is . . . a defining narrative that concisely captures the conclusion of America's twenty years of war in Afghanistan. This book is destined to be the classic against which all other books on this subject will be measured."

—LIEUTENANT COLONEL DAVE GROSSMAN, US ARMY (RET.), AUTHOR OF *ON KILLING*, *ON COMBAT*, AND *ON SPIRITUAL COMBAT*

"Congratulations to my friend Chad Robichaux on his book, *Saving Aziz*. Chad continues to be a true humanitarian for people around the world."

—DAKOTA MEYER, MEDAL OF HONOR RECIPIENT, US MARINE CORPS SNIPER, AND FOUNDER OF OWN THE DASH

"Chad and his team embodied the American spirit in doing the right thing, and *Saving Aziz* captures that spirit."

—MORGAN LUTTRELL, US NAVY SEAL (RET.)

"Chad Robichaux's story is a must-read for every American. The story is riveting, inspirational, and heartfelt in every aspect. This is one book you cannot put down."

—HOWARD KAZANJIAN, PRODUCER OF STAR WARS: THE EMPIRE STRIKES BACK, STAR WARS: RETURN OF THE JEDI, AND INDIANA JONES: RAIDERS OF THE LOST ARK

"If you want a truly patriotic read, look no further. Americans stepping up to do the right thing—that's what *Saving Aziz* is about."

—CONGRESSMAN DAVID BRAT, DEAN OF LIBERTY UNIVERSITY SCHOOL OF BUSINESS

"I am enthusiastic about Chad's book, *Saving Aziz*. Telling this story is another way of bringing healing to those whose wounds are not so easily seen. Chad, thank you for writing this book."

—SI ROBERTSON, STAR OF DUCK DYNASTY

"Chad Robichaux is a man of integrity and action who demonstrates heroism every day. This book, *Saving Aziz*, is a must-read that reminds us that when the situation seems hopeless, there is courage that prevails."

—CHAD PRATHER, HOST OF THE CHAD PRATHER SHOW PODCAST

"*Saving Aziz* is more than just a book. It's a journey of modern-day patriotism that goes far beyond borders."

—MIKE RITLAND, US NAVY SEAL (RET.), NEW YORK TIMES BESTSELLING AUTHOR, AND HOST OF THE MIKE DROP PODCAST

"*Saving Aziz* is an absolutely incredible true story of heroism, purpose, and making a difference against all odds. Read this book. You won't be disappointed."

—JASON REDMAN, US NAVY SEAL (RET.), NEW YORK TIMES BESTSELLING AUTHOR OF THE TRIDENT AND OVERCOME

"This page turner is hard to put down and getting to know warriors like Chad has reaffirmed my faith in humanity."

—Captain Tyler Merritt, US Army (ret.), former air mission commander, CEO and co-founder of Nine Line Apparel, and president of Nine Line Foundation

"*Saving Aziz* is a gripping first-hand account of triumph amid terror, courage and compassion in the midst of cowardice and incompetence, and hope in the midst of despair. It must inspire all of us to better understand our enemies and better serve our allies."

—Lieutenant Colonel Tommy Waller, US Marine Corps Commander (ret.), 3rd Force Reconnaissance Company

"*Saving Aziz* is Chad's account of rescuing his longtime interpreter, Aziz, and his family from Afghanistan following the disastrous withdrawal. This mission, as you'll see in the book, is a true testament that God does not call the equipped; he calls the willing and then equips them."

—David Barton, founder of WallBuilders and *New York Times* bestselling author of *The Jefferson Lies*

"Chad's book, *Saving Aziz*, describes his team's love and persistence in action while in Afghanistan. In the midst of chaos, Chad, his team, and others he partnered with gave hope, dignity, and a new life for so many people. I thank God for Chad's heart of love and care."

—David Eubank, founder of Free Burma Rangers, veteran of the US Army Special Forces, and author of *Do This for Love*

"Now more than ever, we need books like, *Saving Aziz*; a tale of unstoppable resolve fueled by a burning belief in the American Dream."

—Richard McGinniss, chief video director of the Daily Caller

"This is a superb book to understand what happened in the US withdrawal from Afghanistan and what happened in the attempt to rescue innumerable Afghans and other people from an Afghanistan run by the Taliban."

—Jeff Wells, founding and senior pastor of WoodsEdge Community Church

"In this book, Chad Robichaux exposes the very heart and soul of what every Afghanistan veteran experienced as we watched the fall of Kabul. Thank you, Chad, for answering the call to do what is right and for chronicling the story of our generation."

—MAJOR MIKE SIMPSON, MD, US ARMY SPECIAL FORCES (RET.),
HOST OF MIND OF A WARRIOR PODCAST, AND AUTHOR OF HONED

"I highly recommend this book to truly understand what happened—both the good and the bad—and to never forget the history of what a number of us were involved in: seeking to save lives on both small and large scale and doing what most said couldn't be done."

—VICTOR MARX, PRESIDENT AND CEO OF ALL THINGS POSSIBLE MINISTRIES

"Chad Robichaux's astonishing first-hand account of saving Aziz and so many others is just the latest of his feats of incredible courage and selfless service that will inspire, and hopefully be emulated by, generations to come."

—FRANK J. GAFFNEY, FORMER ACTING ASSISTANT SECRETARY
OF DEFENSE UNDER PRESIDENT RONALD REAGAN

"The size, scale, and execution of the mission described in this book is so overwhelming that we must all recognize God's hand in the life-sustaining work that was done. May we all strive to protect the image-bearers of God in a similar way."

—KYLE THOMPSON, FOUNDER OF UNDAUNTED.LIFE
AND HOST OF THE UNDAUNTED.LIFE PODCAST

"From his efforts to stop veteran suicide to the dramatic effort he made to go back to Afghanistan, Chad has made it his mission to save others from darkness and evil."

—JESSIE JANE DUFF, GUNNERY SERGEANT, US MARINE
CORPS (RET.) AND NEWSMAX ANALYST

"Few men have the combination of a mighty warrior with a prayerful heart—Chad Robichaux is that rare man. God is using him in mighty ways—many of which we may never be able to know about. His selfless journey to lead a team to save those that were left behind in Afghanistan is all you need to know about the character of this man. Our nationwide network of intercessors were proud to uphold him and his team in prayer during their multiple missions. Saving Aziz is gripping, raw, inspiring, and full of daring stories that will build your faith that there are still heroes among us."

—DAVE KUBAL, PRESIDENT AND CEO OF INTERCESSORS FOR AMERICA

SAVING AZIZ

HOW THE MISSION TO HELP ONE BECAME
A CALLING TO RESCUE THOUSANDS
FROM THE TALIBAN

Chad Robichaux

with David L. Thomas

NELSON
BOOKS

An Imprint of Thomas Nelson

Published in Nashville, Tennessee, by Nelson Books, an imprint of Thomas Nelson. Nelson Books and Thomas Nelson are registered trademarks of HarperCollins Christian Publishing, Inc.

Published in association with The Howard Literary Agency, 102 Yellowood Drive, West Monroe, LA, 71291 represented by John Howard.

Thomas Nelson titles may be purchased in bulk for educational, business, fundraising, or sales promotional use. For information, please email SpecialMarkets@ThomasNelson.com.

Scripture quotations marked ESV are taken from the ESV ® Bible (The Holy Bible, English Standard Version ®). Copyright © 2001 by Crossway, a publishing ministry of Good News Publishers. Used by permission. All rights reserved.

Scripture quotations marked NIV are taken from The Holy Bible, New International Version ®, NIV. ® Copyright © 1973, 1978, 1984, 2011 by Biblica, Inc. ® Used by permission of Zondervan. All rights reserved worldwide. www .Zondervan.com. The "NIV" and "New International Version" are trademarks registered in the United States Patent and Trademark Office by Biblica, Inc. ®

Any internet addresses, phone numbers, or company or product information printed in this book are offered as a resource and are not intended in any way to be or to imply an endorsement by Thomas Nelson, nor does Thomas Nelson vouch for the existence, content, or services of these sites, phone numbers, companies, or products beyond the life of this book.

Names and identifying characteristics of some individuals have been changed to preserve their privacy.

Numerous pseudonyms used in this manuscript are set in quotes on first reference.

Library of Congress Cataloging-in-Publication Data

Names: Robichaux, Chad, 1975- author.
Title: Saving Aziz: how the mission to help one became a calling to rescue thousands from the Taliban / by Chad Robichaux.
Other titles: How the mission to help one became a calling to rescue thousands from the Taliban
Description: Nashville, Tennessee: Thomas Nelson, [2022] | Summary: "Former Force Recon Marine Chad Robichaux details the incredible rescue missions that evacuated not only his long-time comrade and interpreter, Aziz, but also more than 17,000 Afghans and allies who were left in the grip of the Taliban's violent regime as the United States military withdrew from Afghanistan"-- Provided by publisher.
Identifiers: LCCN 2022012111 (print) | LCCN 2022012112 (ebook) | ISBN 9781400238132 (hardcover) | ISBN 9781400238156 (ebook)
Subjects: LCSH: Afghan War, 2001-2021--Evacuation of civilians. | Robichaux, Chad, 1975- | Afghan War, 2001-2021--Personal narratives, American. | Afghan War, 2001-2021--Peace. | Save Our Allies (Organization)--History. | Afghan War, 2001-2021--Refugees--United States. | Translators--Afghanistan--Biography. | United States. Task Force 714.
Classification: LCC DS371.415 .R63 2022 (print) | LCC DS371.415 (ebook) | DDC 958.104/7--dc23/eng/20220316
LC record available at https://lccn.loc.gov/2022012111
LC ebook record available at https://lccn.loc.gov/2022012112

To the brave Afghan allies who fought courageously alongside us for twenty years, we will never forget the sacrifices you all made for a free Afghanistan and for security around the world. Your sacrifices and dedicated service have earned each of you the right for an opportunity to live free in America, and I am sorry our government has failed you through our broken system. We will never forget you!

To our thirteen brave service members who paid the ultimate price while serving to secure HKIA Kabul, Afghanistan, and the families they left behind.
Lest we forget:
Marine Corps Lance Corporal David Espinoza
Marine Corps Sergeant Nicole Gee
Marine Corps Staff Sergeant Darin Taylor Hoover
Army Staff Sergeant Ryan Knauss
Marine Corps Corporal Hunter Lopez
Marine Corps Lance Corporal Rylee McCollum
Marine Corps Lance Corporal Dylan R. Merola
Marine Corps Lance Corporal Kareem Nikoui
Marine Corps Corporal Daegan William-Tyeler Page
Marine Corps Sergeant Johanny Rosario Pichardo
Marine Corps Corporal Humberto Sanchez
Marine Corps Lance Corporal Jared Schmitz
Navy Hospital Corpsman Max Soviak

Contents

———— ★ ————

Contents

A Statement by the Department of Defense

———— ★ ————

THE VIEWS EXPRESSED IN THIS PUBLICATION ARE THOSE OF the author and do not necessarily reflect the official policy or position of the DoD (Department of Defense) or the US government. The public release clearance of this publication by the DoD does not imply DoD endorsement or factual accuracy of the material.

Author's Note: I submitted *Saving Aziz* for a prepublication security review by the Department of Defense Office of Prepublication and Security Review at the US Pentagon on March 28, 2022. It was cleared and amended for public release on August 18, 2022. All redactions are indicated with a bold, black line over the text so that the reader can clearly see information that exists but is not privy to the public per DoD compliance.

This manuscript was also reviewed by sitting members of the US Congress, as well as active-duty military, retired military leaders from a broad spectrum of military fields to include the Special Operations and Intelligence Communities with ranks as high as four-star generals, and a variety of other individuals familiar with the history, circumstances, and events described in this book. Their reviews, counsel, and contributions give me confidence you, reader, are receiving the most accurate and unbiased truths of the events in *Saving Aziz.*

Foreword by Glenn Beck

───── ★ ─────

I FIRST MET CHAD IN 2016 THROUGH OUR MUTUAL FRIEND David Barton. I heard about his multiple deployments to Afghanistan and his struggles with PTSD and suicide after he came home. Our shared love of history, dependence on our faith to transcend the dark valleys of our past, and desire to use our struggles to pay it forward—these all instantly bonded us. I could tell Chad was the real deal. A man of his word. A man of honor.

I had him on my show several times to share his story and speak on veterans' care, and how his organization, the Mighty Oaks Foundation, was working to combat veteran PTSD and suicide.

Upon hearing about his work, I said, "Sign me up," and my own charity, Mercury One, became a supporter.

We remained in touch, and when the debacle began unfolding in Afghanistan, I didn't give the decision a second thought: Chad and I locked arms and dove in together to do what needed to be done. We did what our government wasn't doing, saving as many people as possible from the bloodlust of the Taliban. Most of these were SIVs, meaning they qualified for Special Immigrant Visas because they helped our country and American troops when they were deployed.

Aziz was one of these. He had been Chad's interpreter on all *eight* of his deployments to Afghanistan as part of a ███ Special Operations Task Force.

Chad says Aziz was more than a fighter against the Taliban—"He was my teammate, and my friend."

When Chad's son Hunter became the third-generation Robichaux to become a US Marine and was himself deployed to Afghanistan, "Uncle Aziz" was there to support him. Aziz also saved Chad's life at least three times, and to this day Aziz's children call him "Uncle Chad." Over those years the two men's hearts were forged together. Two men who came from totally different countries and cultures became brothers willing to die for each other.

Based on his many years of experience in Afghanistan, Chad knew it would be a disaster when President Biden announced that all American troops would be out of Afghanistan by the twentieth anniversary of 9/11. The lives of thousands of SIVs—including Aziz and his family, not to mention American citizens still there—would be in danger from the Taliban as it swept back into power.

Our national honor was on the line, and it was clear it would be forever tarnished if our government was left to its own devices. The irrepressible call of duty once again welled up in Chad's soul. "I have to get my brother," he decided. Costs no longer mattered. Aziz had been loyal to him. Now it was Chad's turn.

When the administration announced that the American withdrawal would take place even earlier, in August, the rescue mission became even more urgent. Chad immediately began contacting friends, many of whom were veterans from the special operations community, to see if they could help. One team member described it as a "task force of the willing." Without hesitation, they agreed. They, too, believed our national honor was at stake.

The rescue effort involved business leaders, politicians, and activity military on the ground in Afghanistan. It led to the founding of a new organization I enthusiastically endorse, Save Our Allies, which to date has rescued seventeen thousand Afghan refugees from the Taliban—including Aziz and his family.

Americans will never forget the harrowing images from the summer of 2021 of Afghans chasing evacuating American planes on the Kabul airstrip. They will never forget seeing bodies fall off those planes as they ascended into the clouds. That's how desperate so many were to avoid the impending slaughter by the Taliban—a slaughter our government was doing little to prevent, despite the fact that so many of the Afghans had helped us for years, even decades.

Thanks to all the supporters of Mercury One and the Nazarene Fund, we were able to help Chad and his team extract thousands of people. It was truly miraculous what they were able to achieve. When I went on air and said we needed to raise $15 million in three days, I thought to myself, "There is *no way* we'll raise this much." But our generous audience upped the ante and raised $20 million in three days, and about $46 million when all was said and done.

But we weren't the people who could actually get these refugees and SIVs out of Afghanistan. We needed people like Chad and his team, who knew what they were doing and were trustworthy. Our group could send in charter flights. But we didn't have a network on the ground that could go in and get people, shelter them, and get them around Taliban checkpoints. We had the planes. But these people needed more than planes to get out of Taliban-occupied territory to safety. They needed experts, heroes, like Chad.

Forty-six million dollars is *a lot of money—sacred* money—and Chad was the first guy we called. What he and other honorable Americans achieved in Afghanistan was a bigger rescue effort than the Berlin Airlift. That was accomplished by the United States government. But this operation was done by private citizens, like the 1940 evacuation of British soldiers from Dunkirk by average British citizens with their own boats and yachts. This was a modern-day Dunkirk.

During those dark, early days, I said something about our country that had never, ever crossed my mind before: "If this is who we are, then I'm more than happy to renounce my citizenship." The way certain people at the State Department acted at times was unbelievable. We were witnessing evil. And when it came to the Taliban, I understood for the first time how Schindler must have felt when, at the end of *Schindler's List*, he wondered if he should have sold even his lapel pin to save one more person.

These refugees and SIVs meant less than nothing to the Taliban. They were going to kill them. It was as if we were pleading with them, "Just give them to us, we'll take them. You don't want them. You hate them. Let us take them from you." And then to see our own State Department obstruct our efforts was *shocking*. Chad's organization deals with this to this day. As he once told me, "As a very patriotic person, I never thought I'd be in the position of apologizing to a foreign nation for America."

But like Chad, while this crisis made me ashamed of our government, it also made me prouder than ever of the American people. I was at a point where I was absolutely *hopeless* about America. I thought, "We're not going to make it."

But when I saw people from all walks of life, all income levels, and all parties come together and say, "This is wrong. *We'll* do something about it!" my heart swelled. Our national honor may have meant nothing to those in Washington, DC. But it meant *everything* to countless Americans.

For the first time in my life, I felt that if government and elites would just get out of the way of *people*, we'd solve a lot of our problems. Previously I had heard about the glory of the average citizen at Dunkirk only in history books, documentaries, and movies. But Chad and our supporters made it possible to witness that same glory with my own eyes.

On June 4, 1940, the last day of the evacuation of Dunkirk, Winston Churchill spoke before the House of Commons and described it this way: "A miracle of deliverance, achieved by valor, by perseverance, by perfect discipline, by faultless service, by resource, by skill, by unconquerable fidelity, is manifest to us all."[1]

The same could be said of Chad and his team.

Dunkirk, while not a victory in the traditional sense of the word, nonetheless galvanized the British people to fight on. In the same speech Churchill also uttered the timeless words we all remember to this day: "We shall fight on the beaches, we shall fight on the landing grounds, we shall fight in the fields and in the streets, we shall fight in the hills. We shall never surrender!"[2]

I hope you come away from Chad's story inspired to keep fighting for the sacred honor of our country—the same honor our founders appealed to in the Declaration of Independence. This country is full of good people, all of whom stood up when we needed them most. They didn't need the government to do the right thing. They did it *in spite* of the government.

The American people are fundamentally good and decent. That is what inspires me, to paraphrase Churchill, to carry on the fight in our schoolhouses, our churches, our communities, our state capitals, and in the halls of power in Washington.

The good are all around us, ready and willing to band together in acts of love, mercy, and sacrifice. I hope you come away from reading *Saving Aziz* with the same hope it gave me, and a renewed conviction that we, too, must never surrender. Our country and its honor are still worth fighting for.

—Glenn Beck

Preface

————— ★ —————

AZIZ OPENED THE DOOR AS SOON AS I KNOCKED.

"Brother!" he exclaimed.

"I'm so happy you're here safe, brother," I said.

I noticed tears in his eyes as we reached out to embrace. Through everything we had experienced together, I had never seen Aziz cry.

My heart filled with relief and joy as Aziz's long, thick arms squeezed me tight. I felt tears stream down my cheeks and, because Aziz is taller than me, I could feel his tears against my forehead. I broke the embrace when I noticed his six kids racing toward me. Mashkorallah—who had pleaded for my help through video messages—latched onto my waist.

"Thank you, Uncle Chad!" he said as he buried his face into my hip. Hearing "Uncle Chad" in his innocent voice broke my composure once more. Tears rushed back as I scooped him up to hold him close.

I spotted Kahtera, Aziz's wife, remaining at the back of the room, per Afghan custom. Her smile expressed a mix of joy, gratitude, and relief.

I placed my right hand in front of my heart, and she returned the gesture.

"Salaam Alaikum," we said to each other.

"Peace to you."

The traditional Afghan greeting seemed appropriate as, finally, after our six years of futile wrangling with the Special Immigrant Visa (SIV) process and more than four months of increasingly distressed phone conversations and WhatsApp messages, Aziz and his family could look forward instead of over their shoulders. In the security and comfort of the humanitarian center in the United Arab Emirates (UAE), they could relax.

In peace.

I had not seen Aziz's family in fourteen years, since my eighth and final deployment in Afghanistan ended. In title, Aziz was my interpreter for every tour. In reality, every step of the way, he was a fighter against the Taliban. More than that, he was my teammate and my brother.

After I returned home, our communications had to be limited for a few years because of my security clearances, but through social media, I could check in on how the kids I'd shared meals and kicked soccer balls with were growing up. And I could see the new children he and Kahtera had added to their family. Then when my oldest son, Hunter, became the third-generation Robichaux to join the US Marine Corps and was deployed to Afghanistan, Aziz messaged me, "Let him know that his uncle is there for him."

Just like Aziz had been for me.

Aziz was a typical Afghan—loyal and carrying a responsibility to protect me, a welcomed guest in his country with a shared purpose of securing freedom for his people and making the world a safer place. Three times, at least, Aziz had saved my life.

And then he needed me to save his.

On April 14, 2021, President Joe Biden announced that all US troops in Afghanistan would be out of the country in time for the twentieth anniversary of 9/11.

Two thoughts immediately came to mind:

This is going to be a disaster.

Aziz's life is in danger.

I needed to get my brother. I *had* to go. And no expense would be spared.

Then the president's deadline moved up to the end of August. As the rescue team I had pulled together began to go to work, we became aware of thousands more—US citizens, Afghans, allies, the vulnerable—facing persecution, and possibly death, if they were not saved from the emboldened Taliban's rapid progression toward taking over the country as our troops departed.

My decision to rescue Aziz mushroomed into a coalition of nonprofits' efforts under the name Save Our Allies. The effort included donors, business leaders, politicians, and even a few active military in Afghanistan confounded by orders from back home. For all, the motivation was the same: we felt compelled to do the right thing for our fellow man.

I began coordinating the complexities of our initial operations, dedicating days and nights to our efforts. While preparing to depart home to establish a command center in Abu Dhabi, I stayed in touch with Aziz and kept him connected with our four-man team working inside and outside the Kabul airport. When I was able to reach Aziz by phone, his tone was different than I had ever heard from him. We'd been through gunfire and rocket blasts together. We'd pulled off escapes with our lives endangered. Aziz was as street-smart and cool as they came. But now, with the lives of his wife and kids at stake, I could tell he was scared.

The Taliban was adding checkpoints throughout Kabul, making it progressively difficult to reach the airport's perimeter. When Aziz's family attempted to approach the airport, the increasing presence of Afghan resistance fighters, random violence, and the thousands of freedom-seekers gathered there prevented them from making it to the gates. On one occasion, we came agonizingly close to getting Aziz's family into the airport. One of our guys was waiting for them at a gate. But as the chaos around them reached deafening levels, the path became even more challenging. When the family neared, Taliban gunfire spooked seven-year-old Mashkorallah, whose piercing cry prompted Aziz to turn the family around and return home. That was their seventh attempt.

That night, Aziz told me he feared for his family because even attempting to get to the airport had become too risky. He didn't think they could make it, he said, but he agreed to try one more time.

Aziz didn't sound hopeful, and I was beginning to concede that I would never see my brother again.

The following morning, on Friday, August 20, Aziz informed me his family had made it to within a hundred yards of a gate—but not the gate we had designated. Sean from our team was waiting for them on the opposite side of the airport.

I informed Sean and added, "They're not going to be able to stay there. We have to get them now."

Sean immediately contacted a small team of US special operators who had offered to help outside the scope of their duties. They drove outside the airport gate, loaded Aziz and family into their armored vehicle, and ushered them through the gate. Moments later, I learned we had saved Aziz through a photo confirmation.

Once safely inside the airport, an emotional Aziz texted me his appreciation.

"Thank God you made it, brother," I texted back. "I've been praying for you and doing everything we could."

"Thank you," he replied. "I can't wait to see you."

When Aziz's family arrived at the humanitarian center a few days later, they were part of the more than five thousand vulnerable Afghans there who were rescued by Save Our Allies. More were coming.

After our warm reunion, I turned to Aziz and said, "We care about you so much because you are so important in our lives. We came to get you, and now all these people are here because of you."

Another pair of tears began streaming down Aziz's cheeks.

What started as one man's desire to save another man's life had become so much more.

Because it was the right thing to do.

And *someone* had to do it.

One

———— ★ ————

Perspective

WANT TO COME OVER TO MY HOUSE AND WATCH THE ELEC-
tion with us?"

Aziz's invitation caught me off guard. Not the offer to come to his
house—in our three months working together, I had grown fond of the traditional Afghan meal of rice pulao, usually with chicken, sometimes with lamb
or beef, that his wife prepared for us. Kahtera and the kids always served the
menfolk bread and tea too. And, without fail, there were sweets for dessert,
although back home we would consider them hard candies.

Then the kids in the house—not only his, but nephews and nieces—were
usually up for kicking a soccer ball around with "Uncle Chad" in the dirt yard.
Or, for the boys, a good wrestling match. Their enthusiasm reminded me of
my own three children back home.

Inviting me to his home was just one of Aziz's ways of taking care of me.
I was on my first deployment to Afghanistan as a Force Recon Marine serving
on a ███ Special Operations ████████████████████████████ task
force in Afghanistan as part of the special operations forces (SOF) community.
Aziz was my interpreter, and my trust in him ran so deep that he remained my
"terp," and more so my teammate, for all eight of my deployments through 2007.

1

My assignments often called Aziz away from Kabul and his family to travel deep into the mountains and remote villages of Afghanistan ▮▮▮▮▮▮▮▮. We often worked as a pair. When we were able to return to Kabul for one of our few short breaks from operations, even though this was Aziz's time to reconnect with his family and even though I lived with my teammates, Aziz showed me hospitality because he knew we were usually having to cook for ourselves. Aziz felt responsible for ensuring I was well taken care of.

What surprised me about Aziz's invitation was the reason: his family was throwing a party to watch the results come in for the 2004 US presidential election. I had learned that Afghans sought any excuse for holding a celebration. Still, Aziz described their election party as we would a Super Bowl party back home.

My teammate Bink, another Force Recon Marine, accompanied me, and we walked into a home packed with people and food. In Afghanistan, when a family gathers, that means the *entire* family because their culture puts the family's needs before the individual. As a family grows, the eldest member adds on to his house so that all the generations live together under one roof.

The US election, though, was a significant enough event to invite friends over too. Kabul was nine and a half hours ahead of East Coast time in the States, so the huge party started during the early morning. I watched Aziz's family and friends enthusiastically support President George W. Bush's re-election bid. In the immediate aftermath of 9/11, Bush had declared war on terrorism, and a coalition of forces led by the United States moved into Afghanistan and, by December, had removed the Taliban from power. Aziz's family was grateful for the president's commitment to maintaining the presence of US and allied military forces in Afghanistan. The primary opposing candidate, John Kerry, had criticized President Bush for diverting military resources from Afghanistan to Iraq. But the consensus fear among Afghans was that Kerry would withdraw all US military from their country and the Taliban would regain control.

Around 10:30 a.m. Kabul time, swing state Ohio was called for Bush. The news that Bush appeared headed for four more years in office sparked an outbreak of hugs and dancing seven thousand miles away from the United

States. Then the party was really on, with the rest of the day filled with joy and laughter and a lot more eating.

As Aziz's family followed the returns, the depth of their passion made me curious. ██ ████████████ Aziz had already taught me enough about Afghan culture for me to blend in as a Westerner who appeared to belong there. But over the next few days, I peppered Aziz with rounds of questions aimed at grasping why the occupant of the Oval Office in Washington, DC, was so interesting to him, his family, and his countrymen. He realized his words could not satisfy my curiosity.

"I'll show you," he said.

Aziz drove me to the eastern side of Kabul, just off the Jalalabad Road that enters the capital city. We stopped at a dull gray, four-story apartment building. The crumbling concrete exterior conceded the building had been neglected. As we walked up to the building, Aziz pointed out scars all over the exterior walls. They were bullet holes, he said, courtesy of Taliban gunfire from 7.62mm bullets. Missing chunks of the building were the result of rockets and explosions. Electrical wires dangled from the walls and nearby poles. The Taliban had ripped out the lines, disconnecting the residents from the Western idols of technology they believed served as a distraction from the highest callings in life—to worship Allah and engage in jihad, the holy war. Cutting off electricity also cut off the residents from the truth available from the outside world through satellite television and radio broadcasts.

Aziz motioned for me to go inside as he explained how under Taliban rule, he had taught English in the basement of that very building. He hid his class and students because the Taliban opposed the teaching of English to Afghans—or anything else the Taliban considered Western, for that matter. Aziz was risking his life simply by teaching English in his hometown. He changed careers when he received an opportunity as an entry-level interpreter with our task force. Aziz had no formal military training, but he decided that if his mastery of our language could keep his country out from under Taliban rule again, he was all in.

As he led me to a stairwell, he told stories of the Taliban storming apartments searching for contraband and possessions banned by the Islamic law (Sharia) they strictly followed and enforced on others. Incredibly, Sharia law permitted them to rape, beat, and kill young girls they caught violating the laws. Numerous girls, Aziz told me, took their final steps up these stairs to the rooftop where they jumped to their death rather than suffer at the hands of the Taliban.

One of those was Aziz's twelve-year-old cousin.

Next, Aziz drove me north of Kabul's center to the base of Bibi Mahru Hill. With its breathtaking 360-degree view of the city, the hill is a popular tourist stop. Our hike to the top was short, only about five hundred yards, but steep. We climbed toward a diving platform that looked out of place for the setting. Aziz told me the Soviets had built an Olympic-sized swimming and diving pool atop the hill in the 1980s, during the Soviet-Afghan War, for their athletes to train at elevation.

When Aziz and I reached the hill's peak, kids playing on the ladders and diving platforms scattered. As we neared the pool, the only sound other than our footsteps came from the gusting wind. Amid the eerie quiet, I noticed a cable suspended from one of the middle diving platforms, about seven and a half meters above the pool. The cable, made of steel, barely swayed in the wind. It ended in a slip-knot noose.

"I've witnessed many public executions here," Aziz said. "Some were hanged; some were thrown off the towers like garbage and died on the concrete floor—and not always immediately."

After the Soviets left Afghanistan following nine years of war, the difficulty of pumping water to the top of the hill to fill the pool wasn't worth the effort for a nation with little interest in training athletes for international competition. When the Taliban seized control of Afghanistan, they found a use for the empty pool.

Aziz and I descended the ladder into the pool's deep end. The width spanned twenty-five meters. The wall was riddled with bullet holes the size of 7.62mm bullets. They were head-high of a person on their knees. And there had to be thousands of holes. I crossed to the shallow end, stepping around puddles left by the latest rain, and observed the same pattern of bullet holes in that wall. They were the height of the head of a kneeling child.

I pulled my Leatherman tool from my pants pocket. With the pointed pliers, I dug into a few of the holes. I removed two bullet jacket remains and looked down at them in my hand. Two symbols of the Taliban's hatred of innocent people. Of unimaginable evil. I slid the jacket remains into my pocket. I didn't want to forget the anger I felt standing next to those bullet holes.

Aziz knew this place would show me why his family was so caught up in our presidential election. My home country was the land of the free. Theirs was now becoming one. They needed us to help bring that freedom to completion for them and for future generations of Afghans.

I returned to that pool—the Killing Pool, I came to call it—numerous times during my deployments. I would sit in the breeze and the quiet and the eeriness and stare at that steel cable. And the bullet holes. I imagined the faces of the innocent people, of the women and kids especially, killed there only because they tasted freedom and discovered a joy so rewarding that they didn't want to go back to their old lives of oppression. They couldn't go back, no matter the cost.

I was in Afghanistan because of 9/11, fueled by a passion for retaliating against the terrorists who killed three thousand of my fellow Americans, against those who, in the name of a political and religious doctrine I could not comprehend, had attacked our God-given freedoms. Brimming with youthful bravado and naivete, I was excited to defend America. I was driven by a patriot's convictions and the certainty that the sort of freedom represented by America and our Constitution must be defended both at home and abroad against those who would take it away, such as the Taliban.

I had joined the ▮▮▮▮▮ task force in 2003 to be part of a group of special operations units from each branch within the United States military who performed ▮▮▮▮▮▮▮▮▮▮ counterterrorism activities. I was laser-focused on my specific mission in Afghanistan. Even though I was in a foreign land, amid a foreign culture, alongside a foreign people, I had spent most of my life focused on my own worldview, rarely thinking of anyone else's. I only barely recognized America's impact globally, much less in Afghanistan. Like many others who served in the US military post-9/11, I just wanted to hand-deliver retribution to terrorists.

The Killing Pool changed my perspective.

I discovered there that America does make a difference in the world, that what we do outside our borders matters because other countries look to us for leadership. They are homes to people much more like us than we realize. We might look different from one another, communicate differently, or look to different sources for faith and hope and inspiration. But what we hold in common unites us despite all those differences: we are all part of the human race, and, ultimately, we just want to live a good life, free of oppression. And those people rely on us to help—and sometimes entirely—protect their freedom.

The Killing Pool changed my purpose.

If I could prevent one teenage girl from choosing to jump from a rooftop rather than suffer rape and abuse at the hands of the Taliban, my time in Afghanistan, however long that might be, would be worthwhile. If I could prevent one family from being forced to watch their father shoved off the highest platform to his death in the empty swimming pool below, I would fight for every member of that family. If I could prevent one child from dropping to their knees inside that pool to be murdered by a monstrous coward, I would give my life for that child.

Before, retaliation had consumed me. Now, my heart broke with compassion for the Afghan people. I had to help. I had to fight for them.

The Killing Pool changed me.

Two

★

Developing a Bond

I WAS ████████████████████████████████ CONDUCTing ████████ logistical operations for my assaulter teams tasked with capturing or killing the highest-value targets of Taliban leaders in the Afghanistan region, getting my guys out safely, and everything else in between. Aziz was my interpreter from start to finish. He had been teaching English in that apartment building when my teammate "Andy" recruited him to our task force. Aziz spoke English extremely well, and as crazy as it sounds, teaching English under Taliban rule was a risky way to make a living.

Aziz was twenty-five years old, married, and knew his country inside and out. He also was street-smart and capable, a necessity for an interpreter in our task force's assignments.

As with all the Afghans hired as interpreters, we brought Aziz in at entry level to allow us time to see him at work and discern how much we could trust him. Interpreters' job descriptions varied depending on the unit to which they were attached. An interpreter assigned to an administrative unit, for example, would be asked only to interpret. But in an infantry unit, an interpreter would also fight alongside our troops. By signing up for special operations, Aziz knew he was taking on a dangerous assignment, but that fit his personality, courageous and passionate.

Of the local nationals working with us, Aziz quickly worked his way into becoming our most capable and most trusted.

Although Aziz came to us with no formal military background, his father had been part of the Afghan army in the 1980s that the Soviet Union helped build up in support of its fight against insurgent groups. Aziz had grown up around fighting from childhood and understood the military mindset.

We fast-tracked Aziz's training. Typically, interpreters on our task force went to an outside country for a ▓▓▓ training program that taught para-military skills. After two to three months of training, the interpreters returned to Afghanistan and received their team assignment. But not with Aziz. We didn't want to wait for him to be trained or risk losing him through an assignment to another team. Aziz was different from the others, and we trained him ourselves. Our command's job was to hunt down the most-wanted "bad guys" on the battlefield, and we made sure Aziz could shoot, communicate as needed, and facilitate everything necessary for building ▓▓▓▓▓▓▓ ▓▓▓▓▓▓ support for SOF missions. Aziz aced every test and passed every lifestyle ▓▓▓▓▓ exam our command gave him. ▓▓▓▓▓▓▓▓ ▓▓▓▓▓▓▓▓▓▓▓▓▓▓▓▓▓ He was a vetted and trusted asset.

▓▓▓▓▓▓ At times I worked alongside other task force team members, but mostly, I was alone, except for having Aziz with me.

Aziz and I traveled into what we called nonconventional or nonpermissive areas, where combat and support forces were not operating. In addition to working in Afghanistan, we worked ▓▓▓▓▓ the Federally Administered Tribal Area (FATA) that blurred the border between Afghanistan and Pakistan. ▓▓▓▓▓▓▓▓▓▓▓▓▓▓▓▓▓▓▓▓▓▓▓▓▓▓▓▓▓▓▓

▓▓▓▓▓▓▓▓▓▓▓▓▓▓▓▓▓

Our purpose was to go into these ▓▓▓▓▓▓▓▓ areas to establish a presence and build SOF missions support for kinetic action, contingencies, and escape. ▓▓▓▓▓▓▓▓▓▓▓▓▓▓▓▓▓▓▓▓▓ ▓▓▓▓▓▓▓▓▓▓▓▓▓▓▓▓▓▓▓▓▓ ▓▓▓▓▓▓▓▓

I was assigned well over a hundred of these missions. No one was beside me, or more instrumental in the success of those missions, as much as Aziz. His skills, expertise, knowledge, and connections made our work successful.

In the United States, a license plate from any of the fifty states allows us to drive anywhere we want to go within the country. But in Afghanistan, specific license plates were required in different parts of the country. Aziz knew the licenses and permits we needed to pass through checkpoints entering those areas. When we traveled where we potentially could be stopped, Aziz was the one who knew—or knew how to find out—the location of checkpoints so we could plot routes around them.

██
██
██████████████████████

Aziz also was my culture expert. I didn't need to try to be an Afghan, but just as I wouldn't want to walk into a gang's territory in a US city wearing the rival gang's colors, I needed to look like I belonged. The first step toward getting caught would be to raise someone's suspicions. ████████████████
██

There was such a thing as being the wrong type of Afghan in the wrong part of town. Accumulating that knowledge would require years of living there. A seemingly innocent activity like driving a car wearing an incorrect piece of headgear would shout, "I don't belong here!" Even if that didn't threaten to expose me, ██
████████ I still would have been susceptible to tribal-based robberies and violence.

Aziz and I continuously operated in environments dangerous to us not only because we were embedded ████████ in Afghanistan ████████ but, by nature of our assignments, because we were in areas where our command wanted to target operating Taliban. We went by ourselves to where the Taliban were, without military support immediately available to us.

We didn't have radios, so we could not call in help if we wound up in a compromised position. I carried an Iridium satellite phone, but those proved a nuisance to operate in the mountains, especially in an emergency. And the uncomfortable reality was, if we were in such danger that we needed to call for help, it would be too late anyway.

Aziz and the other interpreters were representative of the Afghan culture in that they felt a personal responsibility to protect the foreign militaries in their country. Once we saw that an interpreter was committed, that we had mutual regard and concern for each other, we knew he would protect us even at the risk of his own life. Aziz cared about me. He viewed me as his guest in Afghanistan, and as his guest, I was his responsibility to protect regardless of what that might require. Beyond that, I was also his friend.

If we were sneaking our way through back alleys at night, there was no way Aziz would allow me to be the first around a corner. Even though I had more military training, Aziz was going to get ahead of me and make sure the passage was safe for me to enter.

Aziz was fearless. If we had a Navy SEAL team that needed extraction but bringing a quick reaction force (QRF) into a Taliban-infested area would compromise the mission, Aziz and I went to get them. Aziz placed himself in harm's way every time and never questioned it. I couldn't count how many times I saw Aziz save American service members' lives with his selfless actions. He saved mine too, more than once.

Tales from the Road

One time we were staying in a safe house, ▮▮ and I noticed what appeared to be a parade marching down the street toward us. I walked outside and to the edge of the street, sipping on a hot cup of chai, the local tea. This was in 2005, right after a Danish newspaper had printed a caricature of the prophet Muhammad wearing a bomb-shaped turban. The image sparked protests throughout the Muslim world. But I wasn't aware of what had occurred and had no idea this was about the worst possible day for a Westerner to be standing alongside a Muslim protest with nothing but a cup of tea to defend himself.

Aziz was more up on the news than me.

"What are you doing?!?"

Before I could turn to answer that I was watching a parade, Aziz grabbed me and pulled me back into the house.

"Those guys are looking for a Westerner to kill," he told me.

On another occasion, I had hired an American named Jerry to work on one of our operations. Jerry had no idea what we were really doing operationally; he was just happy to have a job and earn a paycheck.

Jerry was alone in his office on a day the Taliban attacked the International Security Assistance Force (ISAF) patrol right next to our office. The ISAF was an international military mission created by the United Nations for training Afghan forces and helping rebuild the Afghanistan government. When the attack kicked off, the Taliban blew a hole in the perimeter wall of our office with a shoulder-launched rocket-propelled grenade. Then a gunfight broke out. The two sides were exchanging small arms and rocket fire when Jerry called me, terrified and begging for help.

I felt responsible for Jerry, especially with him not knowing he was mixed up in ▓▓▓▓▓▓▓ SOF operations. I called my boss and requested a QRF to rescue Jerry. He rejected my request, saying a QRF's arrival could compromise our mission.

"Hunker down and hide in place," I told Jerry. "I'll be right there."

"I'm going to get him," I told my boss.

That statement was met by another big, fat no because it was deemed too dangerous for me to drive through the Taliban-ISAF fight to reach Jerry.

My military experience had taught me that it was better not to respond than acknowledge hearing an order I didn't plan to follow.

"I'm going to get Jerry," I told Aziz.

"Not by yourself," he said. "I'm going too."

Typically, I would have taken the driver's spot, but Aziz beat me to it. When we neared the office, the scene was like right out of a movie. The two sides were shooting at each other and rockets were flying. It was total chaos, yet Aziz drove our Hilux right through the middle of the fight and up to the building. I jumped out and darted inside to get Jerry out from under his desk.

As I pulled Jerry through the front door, Aziz was standing outside providing cover for me while the Taliban and ISAF continued unloading their ammo on each other. Instead of hunkering down inside the crew cab, Aziz was going to make sure Jerry and I made it back to the truck safely. Then he jumped back behind the steering wheel and whisked us away.

Aziz had not met Jerry. He didn't have a personal reason to care about rescuing him. But he knew my chances of going into and out of that fight were much higher if he drove and stood watch outside.

Then there was the time when Aziz and I planned to buy crates of indigenous weapons and ammunition for stocking ▮▮▮▮▮▮▮ for an upcoming operation. We always purchased from local nationals because, obviously, it would not have been good ▮▮▮▮▮▮▮▮ to run around with US weapons. Plus, we were not allowed to stockpile US weapons in an unattended location in an uncontrolled area.

I set up a buy from the nephew of a tribal leader (known as a mullah) who we were spending big money with. I was used to setting up these deals, and this one seemed as ordinary as the rest. Except Aziz sensed something amiss.

One of our previous team members, a Navy SEAL, had made some hasty transactions with this nephew, and Aziz had a hunch the nephew was expecting that same SEAL would be involved in this deal.

"I think they're going to do something," he told me. "I think they might try to rob you, and if they rob you, they'll probably kill you. I don't think this one should be just you and me. I think we should get some more guys to go with us."

I asked two of our teammates, Andy and Bink, to join us.

We drove down a back road to an old, abandoned compound with mud walls. We pulled into an open area in the center, and the nephew came in behind us in an SUV. We closed the compound gate. Aziz and Bink walked over to a lookout point inside the wall to ensure they had a vantage point if anyone else showed up.

Andy spoke pretty good Dari, one of Afghanistan's two official languages, so he engaged the nephew in conversation. Because of Aziz's gut feeling, I monitored the nephew's body language, and he seemed nervous as he talked with Andy. The three of us walked around behind the SUV, and the nephew opened the back so we could inspect the goods. The delivery looked in order: a Soviet-made PKM machine gun, two wooden crates of AK-47s, and a "butt-load" of ammo—military lingo for a lot.

As we checked over the weapons, the nephew grew more nervous and was looking around more than he should have. At the moment I became convinced something bad was going on, Aziz and Bink began yelling to us from the wall.

A car had pulled up with four Afghans carrying AK-47s. They appeared to be Taliban.

That explained why the nephew was so nervous—he expected only Aziz and me to meet him, and he was bringing his buddies into a surprise they wouldn't like.

The nephew started shouting in Dari that the four guys were his friends.

"How do you know they are?" Andy demanded. "What do you have them here for?"

Then Andy grabbed the nephew by the arm and pressed a pistol into his side. I ran to join Aziz and Bink, who had their rifles fixed on the car and were ordering them to stay inside.

We approached the car, pulled the four guys out one by one, and took their weapons. We could have killed them, but they were connected to the mullah, and we didn't want to burn that relationship for future deals. Instead, we zip-tied their hands behind their backs and made them lie facedown in a ditch. Then we moved their car so we could drive out of the compound and tossed the car keys far into an open field.

We weren't so kind to the nephew. We zip-tied his hands and took him with us. Andy drove with Aziz in the passenger seat while Bink and I sat in the back seat with the nephew between us. Bink had a gun in the nephew's ribs, and he was raging mad—barely on the healthy side of panicked, actually—because this guy had just tried to kill us.

The nephew kept repeating a phrase in Dari.

"What's he saying?" an irritated Bink asked.

"He's begging for his life," Aziz said from the front passenger seat.

We did the worst possible thing we could to the nephew: we drove him into town, kicked him out of the vehicle, and went to tell his uncle what had happened. I never saw or heard from the nephew again, so I have no idea what the uncle did with him. But I know what probably would have happened to me if Aziz hadn't voiced his concerns about making the gun buy alone and then wisely positioned Bink and himself overlooking the compound entrance.

We were ▮▮▮▮▮▮▮▮▮▮▮▮▮ eating at a third-world version of a Dairy Queen (minus the Blizzards, of course). We were sitting outside on concrete benches, and I was eating rice and quail. The quail was great, so I was into this meal. Some ▮▮▮▮▮▮ local military were also eating there, and then five dusty Hilux pickup trucks with black-and-white Taliban flags flying in their beds next to mounted PKM machine guns pulled up in front of us. The Taliban fighters unloaded and started walking toward us, still wearing their utility vests with magazine pouches. They ordered food and took seats on vacant benches close to Aziz and me.

The Taliban struck up a conversation with the ▮▮▮▮▮▮ local military—our supposed allies, remember?—saying they had just been fighting with US forces. Watching the two groups talk friendly was nothing new to us. We had been in this area numerous times and drove through Taliban villages the ▮▮▮▮▮▮ local military patrolled. We also routinely came across Taliban going ▮▮▮▮▮▮▮▮▮▮ to fight against Americans ▮▮▮▮▮▮▮▮▮▮▮▮▮▮ ▮▮▮▮▮▮▮▮▮▮▮.

But here we were, ▮▮▮▮▮ Taliban and ▮▮▮▮▮▮▮ US fighters enjoying a tasty lunch together. The situation was strange enough, but then I saw something that really caught my attention. Two of the Taliban fighters, the guys who like to project themselves as tough guys, were sitting together in a chair. One was sitting, legs crossed, on another's lap, holding a Pepsi he sipped through a straw. He draped his other arm around his friend's neck and shoulder, and they held hands with their fingers interlaced.

"Aziz," I whispered. "I have to get a picture of them."

"Don't take a picture, brother!" he whispered back.

"I've got to, man."

"Don't do it!"

I didn't take the picture. Somewhat regrettably.

Three

─────── ★ ───────

Picking Up the Pieces

AS A MEMBER OF THE ▮▮▮▮ TASK FORCE, I SERVED MY deployments in intense spurts with brief recovery breaks. A member of the regular military's deployment, for example, might consist of nine- or twelve-month tours on a military base. In SOF, our deployments were ▮▮▮▮▮▮▮▮ ▮▮▮▮ long, and we were off base for almost all but about the equivalent of one week. Then we would return home, rest up, train up, and jump right back into the same operation.

Aziz and I had plenty of time to get to know each other. When I talk about my time with Aziz, I say that we weren't just teammates—we were close friends who did life together.

With as many operations as we executed, we frequently traveled outside of his hometown of Kabul. We worked long hours planning and doing operations. But we did have time to hang out and just enjoy everyday life.

I got a kick out of introducing aspects of American culture to Aziz through movies and television. Aziz became a big fan of comedian Dave Chappelle, and *Chappelle's Show* was one of our favorite shows to watch. My apologies to Mr. Chappelle, but we bought the first two seasons from a bootleg street vendor in Kabul. We watched the episodes over and over, laughing hysterically and quoting our favorite lines as we traveled throughout Afghanistan.

Aziz possessed a great sense of humor and loved to laugh. He also had a big heart.

He deeply loved his country and took pride in showing me Afghanistan's culture. I'm a history buff and enjoy studying and observing geography, culture, and people groups. Aziz relished being like a tour guide and teacher to me. The more Aziz taught me about Afghanistan and Afghans, the more I understood why nationals like Aziz were so willing to risk their lives serving alongside foreign militaries as interpreters: they hated the Taliban and everything they stood for because of the freedoms they had taken from Afghans.

We were always on the move, and whatever part of Afghanistan we worked in, Aziz knew that area's history. In addition to showing me the popular tourist spots, he took me to places that represented the long history of conflict within Afghanistan. My heart broke—especially after our first visit to the Killing Pool—for the good people of Afghanistan who kept getting caught up in the violence accompanying the perpetual power struggle there.

When Soviet troops invaded Afghanistan in 1979, they joined forces with the new but floundering Afghan communist government. Afghanistan is a collection of tribes, and communism was rapidly dismantling the way of life for the tribes. Many came together to fight back against the communist government and the Soviets. The military part of the resistance's fight was carried out through Muslim guerrillas known as the *mujahideen*, an Arabic word meaning "those who engage in jihad." The word can be used to represent different groups. The mujahideen in this case were the "good Afghans," if you will, fighting for freedom and supported by the United States.

Afghanistan is referred to as the "graveyard of empires" because it has repeatedly brushed back foreign militaries that have invaded the country. After almost a decade in Afghanistan, the Soviets withdrew their troops. I remember as a thirteen-year-old watching the most bizarre video on the news of tanks, single file and amid much pomp, leaving Afghanistan. Soldiers sat atop the tanks, carrying small Soviet flags and waving to Afghans lining the route. The

Soviets had added their name to the list of countries who learned that when it comes to ambitious power grabs, it's best to leave Afghanistan alone.

The Soviets left a weakened Afghan army behind to face the mujahideen alone. With the Soviets removed from the picture, our country held no interest in being involved in the Afghans' civil war. From within the mujahideen eventually emerged what became known as the Taliban. The word *Taliban* is Arabic for the plural of *ṭālib* or "student/seeker." The Taliban were students of a form of Sharia that originated in India in what is known as the Deobandi school of Islamic jurisprudence, although its particular features are by no means restricted to Deobandis alone. The Taliban are strict adherents to this law. They quickly became a powerful and cruel political and military force.

The Taliban began taking over cities and provinces, wresting control of the capital city of Kabul in 1996. The following year it occupied Mazar-e Sharif to the north. Soon, other countries—including Pakistan—began recognizing the Taliban government.

The Taliban's rule, with its strict adherence to Sharia, was characterized by assaults on basic human freedoms. They forced women to remain at home and required them to cover themselves head to toe. They closed schools for girls and banned females from attending universities. Worse, they turned women and little girls into their sex slaves. The prohibition on women going out without a male guardian is not the Taliban's invention. It's basic, mainstream Sharia. The covering of women that the Taliban enforced is likewise based on the Qur'an, which explains that women who do not cover themselves adequately with their outer garments may be abused and that such abuse is justified.

The Taliban carried out violence against ethnic and religious groups that did not share their set of Islamic beliefs, including other Muslim groups. They also allowed other terrorist groups into Afghanistan, including Osama bin Laden and al-Qaeda.

During my initial months living there I heard and learned of firsthand accounts of the oppression the Taliban had placed on the Afghan people. I spoke to good people who had been beaten and permanently maimed and had loved ones killed by the Taliban. Fathers whose children, boys and girls as young as three, had been raped and abused. Little girls who had been forced against their and their parents' will to undergo genital mutilation that deprived them of having sexual pleasure. These are not performed in a hospital but typically in primitive and unsanitary conditions without anesthetic, and the girl is physically restrained against her will. The risks of infection and medical complications are high, and extreme physical and emotional pain often lasts for life. My heart broke for the Afghan people and aligned with their suffering and desire for freedom. As an American patriot I still wanted to fight to protect America, but it was compounded with a desire to protect these vulnerable people from these evils.

The Afghan people suffered unspeakable oppression under the Taliban. Joining the US military and our allies was one way nationals could fight to regain their freedoms—for the freedom to gain an education, to not be forced into becoming jihadist warfighters in a global war against Western nations.

From getting to know Aziz and the tours he gave me around the country, I came to see how perceptions back in the US of Afghanistan—especially of Afghans—were grossly inaccurate. Our military was also at war in Iraq, and the American public seemed to lump the two countries and the two wars together. But Afghanistan was vastly different from Iraq, and from Iran, the country between them on the map.

Afghanistan is not part of the Middle East; it's the crossroads to south and central Asia. Its culture is Asian. With its multiethnic and tribal composition, Afghanistan defies attempts to affix a label onto its people with one broad stroke. The Afghans I met were warmhearted and hospitable. If I were to knock on someone's door late at night and introduce myself as a traveler in search of a restroom or glass of water, they were the type of people who would stop everything they were doing to meet my need. Then they would offer me the opportunity to sit and get comfortable for a bit before resuming my journey or, more likely, invite me to spend the night.

They were honorable and decent people, and they believed that Americans were too. Afghan culture values helping others, and they wanted to help us because they knew we were in their country to help them get rid of the

Taliban and restore their freedoms. They yearned for the education available to all and the pleasures of concerts and sports they once enjoyed.

Americans and Afghans were in sync with the mission—a significant way the war in Afghanistan differed from the Iraq War. We both wanted to eradicate the Taliban for freedom and safety for Afghans, for America, and for the world. As a result, the Afghans were true allies.

Hating the Taliban

I not only heard about the atrocities and oppression the Taliban subjected the Afghan people to, I also witnessed them firsthand. Sometimes I couldn't clear them from my mind.

During my eighth and last deployment, I was ████████████████ conducting a feasibility study for an operation targeting a high-level Taliban leader in the mountains. Aziz flew in to help. While we were there, we got caught up in the middle of a tribal rivalry. We were inside a building when we heard shooting break out from both sides of the street. I looked out to see cars blocking the road, wagons flipped over, and tires on fire for hasty cover as the tribal members fired at each other. It was a rather typical day for such a hostile area, but Aziz and I wanted no part of the action. We scrambled through the back of the building and escaped the area. We completed the study, and one of our special operations teams came in and killed the Taliban leader.

Soon after that successful operation, I took Aziz ████████████████ ██████ home. We were laughing and cutting up the way we always did together when ██ ██ ██ ██ ████████████████████████████████ what I assumed to be a "see you later" turned out to be "goodbye."

████████████████ I was called back to the Persian Gulf to meet with our leadership, and they informed me the Taliban had captured and killed a group of ten Afghan team members who had worked for me. This was a special group to me. I had eaten in their homes with their families and played with their kids.

These guys knew my location ████████████ and possessed the ability to compromise me. The Taliban held them for a week and then hanged them, except for two who flipped to the Taliban side and then turned the others over, causing their deaths. I loved these men; they were my friends. I would have died for them, and they would have died for me. In fact, I believe they did die for me.

Despite being compromised, I decided to return ████████████ and continue on with our operation because I believed its importance was worth the personal risk. A few days after I arrived, I was abducted by ████████████ ██ ████████████████ Taliban sympathizers.

At 5 a.m., I'd heard a knock on my door, and through the window I could see Jack, a guy who had spent time in my home, and an older man. Jack claimed to be Canadian, but he was clearly Pakistani ████████████████████████ ████████. Both were dressed in suits and ties. When I opened the door, two more guys came out of hiding. The four men forced me out of my doorway and into the back of a car. They drove me into the hills outside of town. I thought for certain they were going to kill me, but I was going to put up a hell of a fight when the first gun came out. The men heavily interrogated me for an hour or two, but I held up and, for some reason, they chose to release me.

I attempted one more operation after that, but my mind was not in a good place. I was experiencing severe physiological reactions, panic attacks, and mental disassociation, sometimes feeling as if I had awakened from a dream state. Then, in the middle of my compromised state, our command intel team discovered one of our Afghan teammates, Bashir, had flipped sides to the Taliban.

I had led a group of former Northern Alliance fighters who ████████ ██ worked with our task force. Bashir was one of the guys, and we learned he had provided the information to the Taliban that led to the capture and execution of our ten Afghan teammates. It was a tough blow for Aziz, me, and the rest of my team.

A few days later, my home in Afghanistan was blown to rubble after a vehicle-borne improvised explosive device (VBIED) was driven into my house. Neither I nor any of my team was in the house. A gate guard was there at the time, and I do not know what happened to him. We learned that Bashir had sketched out a map of the home showing the location of our safe and had compiled notes with details such as which individuals slept in which beds and our patterns and times for coming and going from the house.

Our command tracked down Bashir, and a group of our assaulters dropped in to visit him at his home. Literally. Like, with a helicopter and descending on fast ropes. They captured Bashir and threw him in the prison at Bagram Air Base.

The execution of our Afghan teammates, the interrogation, and the attempt to kill me and my teammates shook me up pretty good. My panic attacks and physiological symptoms were progressing rapidly. In a moment of clarity, I concluded my declining mental condition had placed me and others in danger. I needed medical help. I communicated to my leadership over an open phone line that I wasn't feeling well and instead of visiting a local doctor, I needed to see one in the Gulf. That was a signal ▮▮▮▮▮▮▮▮▮▮ that something serious was wrong with me. I booked a round-trip flight to avoid raising suspicions and left behind ▮▮▮▮▮▮▮▮▮▮ all my personal belongings other than what I stuffed into an overnight backpack.

From Misery to Ministry

At the airport leaving ▮▮▮▮ I was paranoid about everyone around me. I noticed more police inside the airport than normal. I believed they were looking for me. I passed through customs with the feeling that I was rolling the dice for my life in a game of roulette, only to make it through and then learn my flight was delayed. I was convinced they were holding up the flight until they caught me. I remember staring at the hands on a clock and feeling like time was frozen.

Finally, we were called to board the plane. To this day I can clearly remember every moment of going through the gate and jetway to walk onto that plane. I don't know if I have ever felt more relieved than when the wheels lifted from the runway and we cleared the mountains.

My leadership held me in the Gulf for four days, I guess to ensure no one was following me. They prohibited me from calling anyone, but I called my grandmother, "Granny," who was like a mother to me. My panic attacks had convinced me I was dying, and I wanted to tell her goodbye. Then I called my wife, Kathy. For the first time since we met, she heard weakness and fear in my voice. Kathy arranged to fly there to be with me, but my command sent some of our team members to our home and shut down her plans of coming over for her safety and to prevent further compromise.

I spent the four days in the Persian Gulf alone. I ventured out to a pharmacy and purchased Valium to calm me down and get me through the flight to the States.

Even at home, I still wasn't mentally right. I was nonstop anxious. My hands and arms would go numb, then my face. My throat would feel like it was swelling shut, and I struggled to breathe. I would feel like I had a thousand-pound weight on my chest.

I met with a psychologist and was diagnosed with severe chronic post-traumatic stress disorder (PTSD). Subsequently, I was removed from the task force and ███████ my program, which removed my access to the classified TS (top secret) SCI (sensitive compartmented information), along with the operations I was participating in. By that point in my career, I had a direct contract with my command, meaning I was no longer on active duty. I essentially was out of a job and home for good. I brought all the anxiety, guilt, frustration, anger, and shame home with me.

Being pulled out of the game without finishing the business of stopping the Taliban and making Afghanistan safer, which I had come to dedicate my life to, made things worse. Nobody understood me, I believed. Everyone was against me. And the toxic mix of thoughts and fears raging inside me was their fault, not mine. I closed myself off to others. All I knew to do was what I had trained to do: fight. But now I was fighting for myself and by myself. And I was losing.

I had trained in martial arts since age five and in Brazilian jujitsu since age nineteen. I also had competed as an amateur and a professional mixed martial arts (MMA) fighter with an unbeaten record. Kathy suggested we open a jujitsu school, and I went full bore into training and running the school. I also returned to fighting professionally in MMA. Within three years, our school grew to two locations and a thousand students, and I still had not lost a fight, had won a world title, and climbed to number six in the world rankings in the flyweight division. I looked like I was winning at everything. But my life was a complete failure.

Kathy and I separated and filed for divorce. I convinced myself the best thing I could do for our three children was commit suicide.

In September 2010, while pressing a pistol to my head, I heard someone outside my apartment door. I hid the gun. When I opened the door, Kathy was standing there. We engaged in a heated argument that led her to ask me a life-altering question: "Chad, how can you do all the things you've done in the military, Afghanistan, be willing to die for your buddies, train so hard for your MMA fights, and show so much discipline to cut weight for competitions, but when it comes to your family, you quit?"

There is no more soul-cutting word to me than being called a quitter. But she was absolutely correct. I had found professional success, but when it came to the most important things like being a husband and a father, and having the will to get well, I had quit.

Kathy was attending church and praying for me, my recovery, and our family. I asked if she could find a man at her church to counsel me and provide accountability. That led to Steve Toth entering my life and leading me to become a Christian. Before then, I would say I was a Christian—I wore a military dog tag that claimed I was one—but for the first time in my life, I surrendered my life to Jesus.

After my recovery, I created a ministry called the Mighty Oaks Foundation to help combat veterans and those from the military communities suffering from PTSD and life issues to move beyond life's hardships and into the life God created us all to live. Over twenty veterans a day were committing suicide, and I felt compelled to tell every struggling veteran I could the lesson I had learned during my journey: in life, just like in combat, we aren't meant to fight alone. With Mighty Oaks, they wouldn't have to.

Four

———— ★ ————

Poor Processes and Bad Decisions

FOR THE FIRST EIGHT YEARS AFTER I LEFT, ███████ AZIZ AND I were forbidden from talking with each other because of the nature of my security clearances. We limited our contact to likes and comments on personal social media posts.

President George W. Bush had launched Operation Enduring Freedom in the aftermath of 9/11. As part of the Global War on Terrorism, Operation Enduring Freedom had two main objectives. The first was to get rid of al-Qaeda, the Taliban, and other terrorist organizations primarily in Afghanistan but also in other countries. The second was to remove Iraqi president Saddam Hussein from power. That operation ended in 2015, and its successor, Operation Freedom's Sentinel, brought a new focus on smaller, NATO-led operations.

With the transition in our military's responsibilities in Afghanistan, I knew parts of the operation I had been involved in were finished. Without being told the restrictions had ended, I felt comfortable reestablishing open communication with Aziz. He was happy we could catch up with each other.

At that time, Aziz expressed his desire to come live in the United States, so we immediately initiated the Special Immigrant Visa process for Aziz and his family, which had grown from three children to six since I had left.

Aziz's SIV process would fall under the State Department, which had the authority to issue SIVs to Afghan nationals under Section 602(b) of the Afghan Allies Protection Act of 2009. The SIVs were designated for Afghans who served as translators and interpreters or for other professionals employed by or on behalf of the US government in Afghanistan. The visa would provide a direct pathway to a green card. This act was an agreement with these Afghans and a promise from the people of the United States that we would support them and allow them to migrate to America. It was a debt we owed to Aziz and the thousands of other allies who served us for twenty years.

The program had faced much criticism long before the 2021 withdrawals began.[1] SIV applicants were waiting an average of two to three years for their applications to be processed, even though Congress mandated that the process take no more than nine months. Only half of applicants were making it through the process. At times, the backlog was as large as the number of total approved applicants. From 2009 to 2019, 18,471 Afghan SIVs were admitted into the United States. As of September 2019, 18,864 applicants remained in process for SIVs.

The SIV system is broken, and even those who successfully navigated the system come with tales of a maze of paperwork, red tape, and hoop-jumping that leads only to redirection or rejection, potentially starting over many times.

We were prepared to do whatever was required and persevere for as long as necessary to bring Aziz, Kahtera, and their children to the United States.

Until 2021.

On April 14, Luke, my media agent, called to ask if I'd heard the news. "President Biden just announced that he's pulling all troops out of Afghanistan," he said.

"He gave a date?" I asked.

"Yes," Luke said. "He wants to be out by the twentieth anniversary of 9/11."

That was terrible news for America, Afghanistan, and Aziz.

I wasn't surprised to hear Biden say he would withdraw our troops. As vice president to President Barack Obama, Biden had shown little interest in maintaining a robust military presence in Afghanistan. During the run-up to the 2020 election and after assuming the Oval Office, he repeatedly talked of decreasing our military footprint there to only counterterrorism efforts, such as special operations forces. President Trump, at the time, was the one telling voters his foreign policy included a complete withdrawal of US forces from Afghanistan. He supported his ambition with an agreement negotiated with the Taliban to have our troops out of the country by May 1, 2021. However, I had a conversation with General Keith Kellogg, then national security advisor, who said President Trump never would have forfeited Bagram Air Base and would have handed it over to the international community with the United States continuing to serve in a support and advisory role when it came to fighting global terrorism and threats to America. Trump's secretary of state, Mike Pompeo, also has stated the same publicly. So, withdrawal of troops from Afghanistan while leaving some sort of contingent to fight terrorism seemed like the one thing Trump and Biden agreed on. Or so it seemed. The important difference was in the details between the two presidents' terms and deadlines.

To be honest and fair, I equally disapproved of both the Biden and Trump administrations for negotiating with the Taliban. But at least the Trump administration established terms the Taliban had to meet for the withdrawal. The Biden administration announced only a date. Setting terms rather than a date is not only a proven negotiation strategy but also common sense in determining who is in charge and has the negotiating high ground.

Trump White House chief of staff Mark Meadows told in his book, *A Chief's Chief*, of a conversation between President Trump and the Taliban's number two, Mullah Baradar, that made clear the Trump administration had a different intention. According to Meadows,

> "Before we start this withdrawal," President Trump said, "I want to make something clear. Let me just tell you right now that if anything bad happens to Americans or American interests, or if you ever come to our land, we will hit you with a force that no country has ever been hit with before—a force so great that you won't even believe it. And your village, Mullah? We

know where it is. We know it's the Weetmak village. If you dare lay hands on a single American, that will be the first thing that I destroy. I will not hesitate."[2]

When President Biden announced America's withdrawal date, we yanked any bargaining possibilities off the table and dunked them in a trash can. We forfeited control of our negotiating power. With the entire world knowing our departure date, all the Taliban had to do was bide its time—what was a few more months after twenty years of being rooted out by us? The Taliban wanted us out and just needed to avoid doing anything to screw up the gift we were willing to hand them: a country for them to rape and pillage.

Our announcing a date without terms allowed the Taliban to develop strategies and begin positioning themselves to do what they wanted as soon as our last flight left Kabul. The date also allowed time for nefarious intelligence agencies like Pakistan Inter-Services Intelligence (ISI)—Pakistan's equivalent to the CIA—to not only help the Taliban's planning but also make plans for their self-serving interests in an Afghanistan free of the US and our allies' militaries.

Of the more than forty nations where the United States had troops deployed at the time, the only comparable scenario would be announcing a withdrawal date without terms from South Korea, an equally nonsensical choice.

As a military guy, not surprisingly, I would have voted against a complete withdrawal if someone from the Biden administration had called and requested my input. But if we were dead set on leaving, as we obviously were, we should have told the Taliban, "Our military will leave when we get all our American citizens out of Afghanistan, when all our allies and everyone else we deem a safety priority are out, and when we have removed all the military equipment we want to take with us. Then, and only then, will we leave, regardless of the date."

We should not have left a country housing the terror threat a Taliban-led Afghanistan posed without protecting our citizens and our assets paid for by US tax dollars. The military equipment alone had cost upward of $85 billion, although that figure has been disputed since first reported during the withdrawal. No price, though, could be placed on the national security interest tied to the equipment's technology.

And then there was the withdrawal date. The selection of September 11 as a deadline was disrespectful to all the families who lost loved ones and first responders during these horrific attacks on unarmed citizens. It was also personally offensive to me and many veterans with whom I talked. We were handing Afghanistan back over to the very terrorists who flew those planes into the World Trade Center buildings, the Pentagon, and—if not for the heroic Americans aboard United Airlines Flight 93—possibly the White House or US Capitol. And, no less, the terrorists would be celebrating victory on the day America solemnly remembered the 2,996 lives lost because of their attack.

From a military strategy standpoint, the date also created problems because it fell during Afghanistan's fighting season. Winters are harsh there, with the cold and snow trapping people inside and limiting transportation, and the "fighting season" begins as soon as the snow in the mountains begins to melt, usually in April. That's when the Taliban works its fighters up for jihad to kill infidels or to receive the reward of going to heaven if they were killed or martyred in jihad. From my experience, they hit peak frenzy in the middle of the fighting season, and it continues until winter returns around November.

During my time of service, we always accounted for the culture when planning missions and, except for imminent operations like a rescue, scheduled campaigns around the fighting season and the Muslim holy month of Ramadan. The US military had been in Afghanistan for twenty years, and it was an indisputable fact that it had been ordered to withdraw from Afghanistan during a time of year when the Taliban was more incited to fight. A withdrawal while their fighters were more docile would have made more sense.

I can only imagine how much more frenzied the Taliban fighters were knowing the hand-over date. They had been unable to stop activities forbidden by their extremist beliefs, like girls going to school; women becoming teachers, journalists, and doctors; Christians emerging from the underground church to go public with their faith; and LGBT communities celebrating the freedom to live their lifestyle. But suddenly, they knew that as of September 12, they were the ones who would be free—free to target the lists of names they had compiled to murder, persecute, enslave, or do whatever they wished with.

Numerous contacts within the military told me President Biden went against initial recommendations of his military and national security advisors in setting the 9/11 deadline. Three weeks later, the president changed the date. I was glad he had listened that it needed to change. But he moved the date in the wrong direction—to August 31.

I was already sensing an urgency to get Aziz out of Afghanistan. But now we faced an even shorter timeline.

An Endless Cycle

I initially felt the need to ramp up efforts to obtain SIVs for Aziz's family shortly after President Biden took office. By the time of his mid-April announcement, we already had three months of heightened frustration added to the six years of seemingly getting nowhere in the process.

During the previous three months, I appeared on national media outlets advocating for interpreters in the SIV program. I had observed two problems for Afghan applicants.

As of February, when President Biden issued an executive order to review the SIV process for both Afghan and Iraqi combat translators, seventeen thousand Afghan translators reportedly sought SIVs to allow them to come to the United States. Counting their family members raised that number to seventy thousand. But that total was not high enough to keep our promise to those who fought alongside us.

Second, we needed a streamlined process so that SIVs could leave the country before our military did. The program consisted of steps that, supposedly, required 503 calendar days to process. Aziz's journey through the system was already over 2,000 days old, and we didn't feel any closer to the end than when we started. Thousands of other applicants were dealing with similar experiences.

The interpreters who served with us were intelligent people, but as Afghans they lacked the understanding of how the US government tends to work. It's almost like the first time through the application process is a trial run to see what the State Department will tell you you're missing. Then you spend time tracking down that paperwork. Then you go back to learn the next document you're missing. The cycle seems endless and designed for failure.

A common roadblock for interpreters was needing a contract proving employment signed by the US military commander under whom they had worked. Especially among the commands of our higher-level units, turnover is constant, and the interpreters needed to find a way to secure a letter from their departed commander. Then consider that some of the applicants had not worked with our military for years, and they had no path to obtain the documents needed for an SIV.

Interpreters like Aziz who worked in ████████████████ special operations programs were officially employed as contractors and not paid directly by our government, so they could not have the required contract number in their application. This created a major problem for many Afghans, like Aziz, who served our military in the most high-risk roles.

When Aziz's contract ended, he received the document needed to apply for an SIV, which included a letter from a major general, but his contract number was missing. Repeated attempts to obtain that number failed because Aziz participated in ████████ special programs, and contract numbers for those programs were hard to come by. Aziz received a case number but was stuck in the endless application cycle.

Every email Aziz sent to the US embassy in Kabul was followed by a reply instructing Aziz to have his supervisor generate a new document for him that included the contract number. That instruction was much easier given than fulfilled.

The application process suffered from a case of the right hand not knowing what the left was doing. The State Department required data that was challenging or impossible to obtain based on how the Department of Defense worked with its interpreters. For six years we had banged our heads against the wall of a system not set up for success. I am not being dramatic when I say that I wasn't sure Aziz—or his family—would live long enough to see the application approved.

The Myth of the "Twenty-Year War"

On July 2, the US military quietly pulled out of its largest military installation in Afghanistan, Bagram Air Base, leaving troops only at Kabul's airport (along with our allies) and at the US embassy in Kabul.

I could not understand why we would commit such a critical strategic error. Bagram is the most strategic military location in the world with its position between Iraq, Iran, Russia, and China. All our enemies would do anything to occupy such a global stronghold, and our giving it away would not only be foolish but greatly weaken national and global security.

Also, the White House and State Department had told US civilians working in Afghanistan that they had time to make plans for leaving the country. President Biden said on camera that we would not leave one American behind. Imagine the shock and fear for those Americans who reported to work at schools, hospitals, clinics, and construction sites and learned that the US military had already left Bagram. Although Kabul is by far Afghanistan's most populous city, many of these workers lived in remote areas and panicked and fled to the Kabul airport or for borders. Some hid in fear. Some are still there, hiding in fear while being hunted like Jews during the Holocaust.

Bagram was the first place I'd flown into when I reported to Afghanistan. Over the years, it expanded from a primitive defense—guarded only by HESCO barriers (dirt-filled cages lined in burlap) and concertina wire my first time there—into a fortified military base with a large airfield. Our best assets and resources were at Bagram, and with its location an hour's drive north of Kabul, the base could have served as the best safe haven and evacuation site for American citizens.

Bagram should have been the last place in Afghanistan our military left, but we departed there first—before evacuations.

Abandoning Bagram cost American lives.

Indicative of how little we seemed to care about working with the Afghanistan army, we also left without informing the base commander. He learned of our departure two hours after our military turned off the electricity during the middle of the night and drove away.[3]

For weeks I had been hearing through my military network that we were leaving Bagram. The world's most powerful military can't up and leave a base like Bagram without some leaks ahead of time. Plus, during the Iraq War and under President Obama and Vice President Biden, the White House chose a similar exit strategy from Al Asad Air Base in western Iraq. Instead of telling the Iraqis of our plans, we packed up in secret and then walked out and handed them the keys. There seemed to be a track record of recklessly leaving a war zone, abandoning Americans and allies, leaving billions of dollars in equipment and technology behind, and creating a vacuum for the most ruthless villains in the region to fill.

While our departure from Bagram was not a surprise, it did occur much faster than I expected.

President Biden's announcement of the amended withdrawal date came two days after we left Bagram. His stance was unmistakable: our future with Afghanistan would consist of diplomatic rather than military solutions. I could almost hear the Taliban laughing.

The Taliban is not a government; it's a paramilitary organization and is still listed as a terrorist organization by the United States and the international community. The Taliban does not understand diplomacy; it recognizes strength and power. When it senses weakness, it tramples over an opponent. Diplomacy is negotiation, and when we didn't show strength, we had no negotiating power with the Taliban because we promised no consequences to fear.

The following day, July 8, in White House press secretary Jen Psaki's daily briefing, she fielded a question about whether the president had plans to mark when all troops were withdrawn from what the reporter called "America's longest war."

Psaki's answer included the comment, "We're not going to have a 'mission accomplished' moment in this regard. It's a twenty-year war that has not been won militarily."

The reporter followed up by asking, "Has this mission not been accomplished?"

"Well, I would say," Psaki began, "we did exactly what we wanted to do."[4]

During her answers, Psaki expressed gratitude for the military members' service in Afghanistan. But I am in constant contact with many veterans through our Mighty Oaks Foundation, and the veteran community viewed those remarks as a slap in the face to the two decades of work in Afghanistan that our military had given to our nation and the world.

The veterans I spoke with refused to accept that the Afghanistan military effort would not be considered anything short of a complete victory. Our nation sent us there to capture and kill those responsible for 9/11, and we did. We took out bin Laden. We removed al-Qaeda as a threat in our homeland. We made the Taliban pay for its support of terrorism against us. We made stabilizing Afghanistan and that area an international effort, bringing in NATO to train and support the Afghan military. We did what we needed to do. We made the United States and the world safer. Then, for political reasons, politicians in Washington spun that mission into something else—nation-building. They tried to make Afghanistan—a unique place with unique challenges—embrace our style of government. And because it sounded good politically, the politicians removed the one element that had succeeded there—our military. Now, the United States and the world are no longer as safe as they were before our military left, and neither are the people of Afghanistan.

I told veterans discouraged by the press secretary's comments, "Despite what the White House says, they don't get to declare what is the victory. We won."

Mission accomplished.

The notion that Afghanistan was a twenty-year war is also extremely unpopular with veterans.

I am convinced Americans were intentionally led to believe we were in a twenty-year war in Afghanistan—an endless war, it sometimes was called— and that we had to pull out completely.

That was a big lie. We were not in a twenty-year war.

Our presence in Afghanistan had shifted to a support and advisory role to the Afghan National Army (ANA) and the Afghan National Police (ANP). And we weren't the only nation in that role either. We were the leaders of a collaborative effort. I have struggled to find another time in recent history when such an international coalition was working together; the results occurring in Afghanistan should have been allowed to speak for themselves.

President Obama declared the end of our combat mission there on December 28, 2014. But it wouldn't be difficult to stir up a good debate on exactly when we practically transitioned from war to the support and advisory role. Perhaps a lack of public consensus on when the transition occurred, or at least discussion of the shift, led to the belief we were involved in a twenty-year war.

For me, the recognition that we were no longer in a war came in April 2017 when President Trump gave our military the green light to drop a MOAB on a large ISIS tunnel-and-bunker complex in Nangarhar Province near the Pakistan border. The MOAB officially is the GBU-43/B, or Massive Ordnance Air Blast bomb. It's more commonly known as "the Mother of All Bombs." At thirty feet long, weighing 21,600 pounds, and with a force equivalent to eleven tons of TNT, the MOAB was our largest non-nuclear bomb. We had never dropped one on a battlefield. More than ninety ISIS fighters, including top leaders, died in the blast.[5]

The message the MOAB sent was that if the Taliban attacked Americans, they would feel the full force of the US military's arsenal. That message, approved by the Trump administration, was different from our approach under the Obama administration.

The ROI on ROE

President Trump's decision to no longer hold back our military showed how changes in the rules of engagement (ROE) from one administration to another affect our military.

A study of the number of US military personnel and civilians killed and wounded in Afghanistan over twenty years and four presidents reveals how vastly different leadership and ROE from the White House affect the outcome of combat and preserve the lives of US service members, which also aligns with civilian casualties.

During President George W. Bush's time as commander in chief, 630 troops were killed and 2,645 wounded in Afghanistan. President Obama's tenure resulted in 1,758 troops killed and 17,592 wounded. President Trump was in office for only four years, but the results of his firm stance toward the Taliban and immediate changing of ROEs to favor US forces resulted in only 64 troops killed and 425 wounded.[6] After we dropped the MOAB, attacks on US troops nearly came to a halt. This positioning and strength not only saved American military lives but made Afghanistan and the world a much safer place.

The truth is that in 2017 we stopped conventionally fighting in Afghanistan and handed that over to the ANA, and we remained in a support and advisory role. We had special operations going out, but we do that around the world anyway and always will. Yet mainstream media narratives have become so good at politically motivated partisan propaganda, and all spun Afghanistan in such a way that it would have been difficult for anyone to conclude anything other than "it was time to pull out of an endless war," "we would have had to leave eventually," and "the withdrawal had to happen, but we could have done better." All lies intended to mislead the American people.

Can we at least ask why the US military needed to leave Afghanistan? Especially considering we had only 4,000 troops (2,500 at one point) there participating with the rest of the international community to support and advise the ANA in fighting the Taliban on their soil to combat global terrorism (and it was working). Afghanistan is far from the only place we have troops deployed. We have 55,165 in Japan, 34,674 in Germany, and 26,184 in South Korea. So why was Afghanistan such a big issue? Why the rush to recklessly move 4,000 troops out with no plan?[7]

I admit that I view our twenty years in Afghanistan through a lens of military strategy. But statements like "It's an endless war" and "We had to pull out" are just not true and are inconsistent with our position around the world.

I heard supporters of our withdrawal say, "We can't keep killing America's sons and daughters." The truth is that every time we lose a service member, regardless of their location or whether it was a combat death, it hurts. I've lost dear friends over the years in Iraq and Afghanistan, and I don't want any of our service members to die. But we do not have a draft in this country. Our military force is all volunteer, and everyone who signs up does so knowing they could lose their life in service to their country and in the necessary defense of those around the world who cannot defend themselves. When we join the military, raise our right hand, and commit to an oath to defend the Constitution against all enemies foreign and domestic, we do so in a conscious decision considering that risk. That doesn't mean we take a flippant approach to casualties. But there is another familiar saying that has merit: we can fight them over there or fight them over here. Because of 9/11, we went to war in Afghanistan to take the fight to the Taliban on their soil to keep it far away from American soil. Then, more recently, we took on our support and advisory role so we could keep the fight over there.

The "twenty-year war" had ended well before it reached year twenty. The "endless war" was over. If Americans had been told the truth by the mainstream media and our government about how our troops were carrying out the mission now in Afghanistan, I believe more would have agreed that it was in the best interests of our country to maintain a small military presence in Afghanistan alongside the rest of the international community. We needed to keep the Taliban at bay there.

The world became a less safe place the moment America announced our withdrawal at the cost of human life and rights.

Five

———— ★ ————

Who Surrendered to the Taliban?

BASED ON REPORTS I HEARD FROM CONTACTS IN Afghanistan, the Taliban seemed emboldened following the United States' date-not-terms announcement. The Taliban was starting to sweep its way across the country, with Kabul its winner-take-all target.

Although we were still committed to the SIV process for Aziz's family, the situation on the ground was more severe than we were hearing back in the States.

I called Congresswoman Vicky Hartzler, a member of the US House of Representatives from Missouri and a wonderful woman and leader. We had worked together through Mighty Oaks Foundation on policy related to faith-based solutions for veterans' care. I informed Representative Hartzler of the incredible service Aziz had provided our country and that although he had reapplied for SIV status on July 1, 2021, he could not get into the US embassy in Kabul because of COVID-19 restrictions.

"We have to help this guy," she told me.

Representative Hartzler committed to doing what she could to push along his application. Although I trusted her, I had no faith in the actual SIV process. I knew that I needed to go into Afghanistan and bring Aziz and his family out.

My teammate Andy and I had already been discussing possible options for saving Aziz. At the end of one of our phone calls, I said I wanted to move forward. Andy immediately said he was on board. Andy and I had stepped in when the government failed once before. In 2005, when Hurricane Katrina wiped out New Orleans, the high winds had destroyed all the city's communications towers on the roof of the fifty-one-story Hancock Whitney Center, or One Shell Square, as it was known at the time. With limited police available and no communications, federal agents went in to secure the building but came into armed conflict with local gangs and were forced to pull back. I had been home from Afghanistan for one day when I received a call from Andy saying the Department of Homeland Security had asked for his help and he needed me to put a team together while he got the equipment and logistics in order. About twelve hours later, we stepped into New Orleans with an eight-man team. It looked like a Third World war zone, with human bodies lying in the streets and sheer destruction to the city's infrastructure. Over the next ten days, we conducted route reconnaissance to plot routes in and out the city, cleared all fifty-one stories of the building and secured it, and were able to clear the roof to land a helicopter with engineers and communication equipment to get communications back up for emergency services in the city. It wasn't much of a break from Afghanistan, but our team was proud we could step in and help.

Now, Andy and I again felt a duty to step up and help our government. We put together an initial plan to save Aziz that we knew could work: using a cover as working for a media organization to get into Afghanistan.

I pitched the proposal to Richie McGinniss, a journalist with the *Daily Caller* who had interviewed me for many stories about Mighty Oaks and veteran issues. I had enjoyed working with McGinniss; I respected him, and like me, he loves a little adventure. He also had recently done some pretty crazy undercover work in producing national stories, including posing as an Antifa and a BLM member to capture much of the footage aired on *Tucker Carlson Tonight* and on Fox News. McGinniss was even right in the middle of the Kyle Rittenhouse shooting, providing medical help to Joseph Rosenbaum immediately after he was shot. You might have seen him testify during the televised trial.

I described for McGinniss how his organization would be our cover by saying they were working on a story out of Afghanistan regarding the withdrawal. They would hire me as their consultant, Andy as head of security, and Aziz as a local culture expert. After getting what we needed in Afghanistan for our piece, we would fly by private jet to Dubai for completion of the production work, but we would need Aziz and his family to accompany us to be interviewed for the story. Then Aziz and his family would remain in Dubai and, of course, never return to Afghanistan. McGinniss was all in for both the story and to get Aziz out, and his bosses at the *Daily Caller* granted our plan an enthusiastic green light.

I crunched the numbers and estimated our operation would cost $65,000.

I believe God has impeccable timing on how He orchestrates events. That same day, I received a call from Wayne Hughes Jr., a dependable friend, advisor, and longtime generous supporter of Mighty Oaks. Wayne had read an article about an Army Special Forces guy who wanted to get his interpreter out of Afghanistan. Wayne wanted me to read the article because the guy was raising money through GoFundMe, which is not the most-trusted means of fundraising. Financial supporters tend to be more comfortable giving to a 501(c)(3) IRS-regulated nonprofit organization.

"Do you know this guy?" Wayne asked. "I want to help with this Afghanistan thing, and I'm thinking about giving to this."

"I don't know him," I told Wayne. "But I'm actually wanting to do the same thing for my interpreter, and I was literally planning it as you called."

"Why didn't you tell me?" he asked.

I explained how I appreciated everything he had done for our foundation over the years and didn't want to ask him for anything more.

"Well, how much do you need?" he asked.

"About $65,000," I replied.

Wayne responded without hesitating.

"Done."

A Reason Not to Fight

First, Zaranj and Sheberghan. Then Kunduz, Sar-e-Pul, and Takhar. Then Badakhshan, Baghlan, and Farah.

Afghan cities and provinces began falling to the Taliban like a drumbeat steadily increasing in tempo. Some of the earlier locations seized offered little to no resistance. They were remote areas with no foreigners, populated only by people groups who had lived there in the same manner of existence for hundreds, sometimes thousands, of years. Taking control of those places would have meant nothing more than driving a pickup down the road and stopping only long enough to raise a Taliban flag.

On August 11, the media reported that one US official admitted Afghanistan could fall to the Taliban within ninety days.

ANA fighters in outer provinces were giving up and leaving their weapons behind for the Taliban to collect. Frankly, it was difficult to blame the ANA because when the United States stopped providing military support, particularly air support, the outcome was determined. ANA fighters were not away on deployment. Their families lived there, and their first priority had to be to protect their wives and children after being abandoned without cause by the country they had fought alongside for two decades.

Since the ground war ended for the United States and we transitioned into our support and advisory role, we and our allies had helped keep the Taliban pushed into the mountains through our air support and handed the conventional fighting responsibility to the ANA. That's where our relationship with the ANA had worked almost flawlessly. For example, if the Taliban felt brave enough to send out a convoy, an ANA patrol could alert us that it had spotted five Hilux pickups carrying Taliban armed with RPGs and mounted PKMs. We would verify the target and then use a vector gunship—fixed-wing or helicopter—or a Predator drone to drop a Joint Direct Attack Munition and erase the convoy from the planet. Or if our military determined the convoy was returning to its mountain home, we could follow the Taliban and bomb the cave they drove into.

We were winning the war on terror because the Taliban knew not to stick their heads out too far. As a result, much of the fighting occurred up in the mountains, where the ANA could pursue the Taliban instead of having to take a defensive stance in more populated areas. Yet a common theme coming from some political leaders in DC and the mainstream media was that the Afghans didn't want to fight for themselves. Because of that, they asserted, there was no reason for us to be there.

Now, with the Taliban once again empowered, that narrative grew louder.

What an insult to the Afghans' warrior culture. The politicians and media members making false claims to advance their political agenda essentially called the Afghans cowards.

Elitist politicians clearly have no clue who the Afghan people are and what they have sacrificed. They didn't get the privilege of fighting shoulder to shoulder with Afghan patriots who risked everything to secure a free Afghanistan and to bravely protect an America they never saw for themselves. My friends and I fought alongside them. They weren't cowards; they were brave Afghan warriors—warriors like Aziz. The truth is that the numbers fail to support claims of Afghans' unwillingness to fight. According to one report, at least sixty-six thousand Afghan troops have been killed since 2001. More than forty-eight thousand civilians also lost their lives, and at least seventy-five thousand others were injured. The report added that those totals could be underestimated.[1]

Amid significant losses, the Afghans demonstrated over two decades their willingness to fight for their country, both when the United States was in the lead combat role and when we dropped back into our support and advisory role. But the ANA was now alone in facing an emboldened Taliban receiving support from Pakistan's ISI, al-Qaeda, and, most would conclude, even Iran and China.

Back in June, the Taliban had captured twenty-two commandos from an Afghan Special Forces unit in the northern Afghan city of Dawlat Abad. As the men tried to surrender, the Taliban made a public display of executing all of them, one of the many atrocities the terrorist regime had committed after the United States announced its withdrawal. I watched the video. A stronger message, though, came in the lack of a response by the United States. Twenty-two of our allies, special commandos we had trained, were executed, and we said and did nothing. We had determined our direction, and the ANA fighters concluded we had abandoned them. They were correct—we most certainly did.

They knew they could not win without us, and, most disturbing, we knew too.

What Americans who have not served in Afghanistan may not understand is the difference in risks Afghan fighters faced compared to our troops. A US service member risked his or her life in Afghanistan. An Afghan risked not only his own life but the life of every member of his family. Thus, facing a no-win scenario, those who walked away were doing so to take care of their families.

On August 12, with the Taliban taking over so quickly now that they faced no resistance, the Pentagon announced the deployment of three thousand US troops to immediately evacuate diplomatic personnel from the US embassy in Kabul. Not that a defeat would have been admitted, but sending troops in after declaring the withdrawal of our military had to be the last thing the White House wanted to do. The withdrawal wasn't transpiring as planned. Unfortunately, the mounting problems were so predictable.

The following day, Kandahar fell. The next, Mazar-e Sharif. The capture of Afghanistan's second- and third-largest cities on consecutive days revealed the Taliban's military strength because the ANA still maintained an operating base in Kandahar. The Taliban had to go into those places with a militant force intimidating enough to compel resistance fighters to surrender.

During that month, our military was monitoring the Taliban's every move. ██
██
██
██
██
██
██
██████████████████

Ninety days? No way. It was clear the Taliban would own Afghanistan in less than a month.

Bashir's Return

With the Taliban's takeover imminent, my concern for Aziz's life, on a 1–10 scale, climbed to 9.

If he had been alone, I would not have worried as much because Aziz could find a way to evade the Taliban and get to a safe location. But he had his wife and six kids with him. And when Aziz and I communicated, his usual steady tone was missing. He was scared for his family.

The velocity behind the Taliban's momentum forced us to repeatedly adjust our plan of going into Afghanistan with the media story cover. We found a potential work-around for obtaining a business visa for Aziz as his reason for wanting to live in the UAE. To provide legitimacy for the business visa, Aziz needed a stand-up company in Dubai. The project's cost kept rising. But each time the dollar amount increased, someone compelled by Aziz's story stepped forward to offer a donation, including Dave Barton and Rick Green from WallBuilders. Another friend kicked in $100,000, giving us a $185,000 budget for saving Aziz's family.

The media attention on Afghanistan forced the Taliban to try to control its mob, if you will. The Taliban had become more PR savvy, and they knew all they needed to do was run out the clock and the country would be theirs. They could claim that the execution of those twenty-two commandos in Dawlat Abad was part of war. But killing innocent civilians was not, and if reports and videos of the Taliban killing women and children got out, that was perhaps the only thing that might cause the United States to delay its withdrawal.

But controlling barbarians is no easy task.

Atrocities were being handled discreetly by Taliban standards. But the Taliban was known to be systematically seeking out interpreters and other allies for interrogation. Some were killed. Aziz told me that one interpreter had pleaded for help getting out of the country because the Taliban had threatened his life. He was out driving with his young son one day and came upon a Taliban checkpoint. Knowing his fate if he stopped, he sped through the checkpoint. The Taliban shot up his car to stop him. Then they pulled him out of his car and, with his son watching, cut off his head.

Aziz's greatest fear was that the Taliban would take his wife and kids and force Aziz to watch as they raped his daughters. Only then would they kill Aziz.

Aziz had achieved a high profile around Kabul. We paid interpreters well, and his business smarts had allowed the companies he ran after I left to be profitable. His natural leadership made him a respected figure in his community, so he was easy to find.

Plus, Bashir, the person responsible for the execution of my ten Afghan teammates and the bombing of my house, had been freed. He had become a Taliban leader and now targeted Aziz.

During the Obama administration, prisoners of war were usually released to Afghanistan, and Bashir transferred from the Bagram Air Base prison to the Pul-e-Charkhi prison in Kabul. He served five years there. As Aziz tells the story—and his anger is still evident when he tells it—when Bashir was released, some Americans gave him money and shipped him to Saudi Arabia.

Aziz balked.

"You guys could have killed him," Aziz said.

"We don't kill people like that. That's not in our rules," came the reply.

"But he's one of the bad guys," Aziz countered. "He told everything about our operations to the Taliban."

Aziz was assured that Bashir was sent out of the country so he couldn't reveal more information.

As the Taliban started capturing provinces, Aziz received an alert from a friend who recognized Bashir among the Taliban. Bashir was now a Taliban commander. Aziz knew Bashir would seek revenge for Aziz's role in his spending six years in prison.

"They are headed to Kabul," Aziz's friend warned. "You need to change your location."

Aziz contacted me to tell me about Bashir and said he and his family were on the move, staying in a different house every night. They lived out of their backpacks, and I spoke to him daily to keep posted on their status and movements.

As good of a plan as our media cover was, it was no longer feasible. Aziz's family didn't have that much time.

Securing SIVs for Aziz's family remained Plan A, but I held out no hope for those chances. We didn't need a Plan B—we needed a *second* Plan A. And that plan was to go save Aziz and his family.

Saigon All Over Again

Afghan cities had been falling for weeks, and the Taliban was systematically taking control of the country province by province and city by city. Even a casual news observer could see the fall of Kabul on the horizon.

I received a highly redacted unclassified document leaked from inside the White House from a National Security Council meeting dated August 14, 2021, at 3:30 p.m. EST. The document revealed that the Biden administration still had not established an actionable plan just hours before the takeover of Kabul. They had not even decided on transit points for those evacuated, known as "lily pad" locations, or third-party countries. Decisions were still being made at the very last minute with lives in the balance (the document is now public).[2]

The Biden administration was advised multiple times from various sources that the Taliban were rapidly sweeping the country. "On the 13th of July [2021], we offered to work with them to help evacuate our partners," recounted former CIA officer Matt Zeller. "We all saw this disaster coming before the inevitable occurred. They didn't get back to us until Aug 15, the day Kabul fell."[3]

This poor planning would result in thousands of American citizens and tens of thousands of Afghan allies left behind. Thankfully, our team and other competent NGOs had devised actionable plans prior to the Kabul takeover, despite the White House ignoring warnings from our intelligence agencies and having no plan of their own. While we don't need the National Security Council documents to tell us the administration was unprepared, the documents reveal the truth and contradict what the White House was reporting to the American people.

The results of the White House not having a plan unfortunately manifested in the events of Sunday, August 15, a sad day in the histories of both Afghanistan and the United States. The Taliban took over the capital city of

Kabul that day with no resistance, President Ashraf Ghani fled the country (hauling possibly close to $170 million with him, we later learned), and the Afghan government collapsed. Afghans flocked in the thousands to the Kabul airport looking to escape.

Also that day, the American flag flying over the US embassy in Kabul was lowered and the embassy evacuated. Hearing the news of the evacuation took me back to meetings in which I participated ████████████ during my time in Afghanistan. I stood inside that embassy complex and proudly watched our nation's flag fly. One of my most cherished keepsakes is an encased flag that flew over the embassy in my honor on March 9, 2006, during Operation Enduring Freedom. On that day, Aziz and I went out to assess an operation to capture a high-value target. When we returned from the operation, I was presented that day's flag. I display the flag on the wall behind my desk in my home office. My heart breaks knowing the honor afforded me is now tarnished by such a disgraceful end to twenty years of fighting terror and making the world a safer place.

To this day, I still wonder how the person responsible for taking down our colors felt as they lowered our flag for the last time at that embassy. I can imagine that person rushing out onto the embassy grounds and hastily lowering the Stars and Stripes.

Here in the United States, on the same day videos circulated of helicopters landing at the embassy as part of the evacuation, Secretary of State Antony Blinken made the rounds on Sunday morning television shows declaring, "This is manifestly not Saigon."[4]

In 1975, the US military pulled out of the Vietnam War, but diplomats, contractors, CIA employees, and Marine guards remained behind. When North Vietnamese troops took over the South Vietnam capital city of Saigon, a hurried, mass evacuation of Americans began. The final Americans in Saigon were forced to evacuate via helicopters landing in the embassy's parking lot and on the roof.

The word *humiliating* is often used to describe that moment in US history.

Five weeks before we evacuated our Kabul embassy, President Biden had assured Americans there would be no such repeat of history.

"There's going to be no circumstance where you'll see people being lifted off the roof of an embassy of the United States from Afghanistan," he said.[5]

Kabul was Saigon all over again.

Contacts on the ground were telling me the Taliban had surrounded our embassy and weren't allowing our personnel out. Embassy workers could not get into a car and drive the four miles to the airport. They had to be flown out via helicopter.

How we left the embassy proved the Taliban was calling the shots, and they knew it. We did not hand over the embassy to the Taliban. No diplomacy was involved. Helicopters flying off a roof is not a peaceful transition; that is a retreat.

The Taliban took our embassy from us.

That was among the fallout of giving a date rather than terms. If our president had said we would leave Afghanistan once we had safely brought out every person on our list—Americans and others—our military could have told the Taliban our embassy personnel were leaving by caravan for the airport and if one of their fighters as much as looked at us the wrong way, our caravan would be the last thing they saw. Clearly, we were not in negotiations with the Taliban. Or, if we were, we had lost control of negotiations.

One of the first edicts the Taliban gave when moving toward Kabul was for the provinces to give them a list of all women from fourteen to forty-five years old so they could be married off to Taliban fighters. Power, control, and war plunder are the earmarks of the Taliban.

August 15 was a day of defeats. Afghans lost their country to the Taliban. For Americans, our military did not suffer defeat, but the US government, with blood on its hands, lost to the Taliban.

And it was a day of dishonesty to the American people.

We were lied to.

Six

───── ★ ─────

Answering the Call

AS RAPIDLY AS THE SITUATION IN AFGHANISTAN WAS SPI-raling out of control, an effort to save Aziz was coming together in equally stunning fashion—so quickly that it could only be described as "a God thing" orchestrated in a divine way I could not explain.

Andy and I started connecting with our network of operators who might be interested in going to Afghanistan with us. We specifically wanted guys who had deployed to Afghanistan, were from the special operations community, had real-world ██████████████████████████ SOF experience, and, most importantly, had a heart to rescue vulnerable people instead of look to get in a fight with the Taliban to sow their war lust oats.

We ended up quickly assembling a core group of operators who were highly experienced, trusted, and rightly motivated. Each would bring something unique to the team. During our initial planning conversations, one said he was aware of 3,500 orphans who needed to be rescued.

We realized then that we had the skills, the ability, the know-how, the experience, and the connections to bring in the resources to help in a way that far surpassed Aziz and his family. We all agreed we had to help as much as we could.

When I created Mighty Oaks back in 2011, God had placed a yearning in my heart to help veterans the same way I had been helped following my PTSD diagnosis and internal battles. The mission He gave me was clear, and we had not veered outside of our scope during our ten years of ministry. Jeremy Stalnecker—my number two at Mighty Oaks and a former Marine infantry officer—is a mission-focused leader, and he has standing permission to rein me in if I start drifting from the specific lane God has called us to run in. When opportunities came to us that were not perfectly aligned with our mission, we closed the door each time. Some would have been really cool work to be a part of. For some of the opportunities we turned down, we supported the work of those who accepted them.

But this Afghanistan matter was different. The "I've got to do this" compulsion was the exact same as when God led me into starting Mighty Oaks. I talked with Jeremy and then our board of directors.

"I have never felt derailed since we started this ministry," I told them. "But I feel God has placed this burden on my heart to do this thing in Afghanistan the way I felt for Mighty Oaks. We, as Mighty Oaks, have to do this."

A couple of board members said they had the same urging in their hearts.

"It's the right thing to do," Jeremy added.

God started bringing groups of like-minded people together, and we began consolidating our efforts.

One such person was Sarah Verardo, whom I met through Mighty Oaks. Sarah's husband, Michael, was catastrophically wounded by two separate IED attacks in Afghanistan in 2010. The blasts took Michael's left leg and much of his left arm. He has endured more than a hundred surgeries plus years of speech, visual, physical, and occupational therapies for his body and traumatic brain injury. Sarah became a champion for wounded veterans and their caregivers through volunteering with The Independence Fund. She eventually became the fund's first CEO. In addition to the direct help The Independence Fund provides wounded veterans and their families, Sarah has become an effective influencer in Washington, DC, of national policies related to military and veteran causes. As I worked parallel efforts in DC through Mighty Oaks, Sarah and I joined forces over the past four years to impact veterans' health-care policy, such as President Trump's executive order creating

PREVENTS (President's Roadmap to Empower Veterans and End a National Tragedy of Suicide), and were together in the East Wing of the White House during its unveiling in 2019.

The trust we gained in each other then led to our creating Save Our Allies as a combined campaign to engage in evacuations from Afghanistan. Getting to that point consisted of a flurry of activities: building a team to go to Afghanistan, establishing a Joint Operations Center (JOC) in DC, raising financial support, fielding requests for people to evacuate from Afghanistan, making media appearances to raise awareness of the need for our operation and others like ours, and setting up Save Our Allies as a nonprofit.

The month of August was a chaotic flurry of planning. Everyone who joined in our effort made more sacrifices than could ever be communicated. For me, much of my August consisted of twenty-hour days and seven-day weeks. I don't know how little sleep the others were getting during that stretch—perhaps less than me—but I was proud to be working alongside fellow Americans driven to do the right thing for fellow humans whose lives were at stake.

Initially we had no intentions of turning Save Our Allies into an independent organization. But our work grew so big and so fast that we had to. We didn't need to put much thought into our name. When anyone heard the name of our campaign (and later our nonprofit), they would know everything we were about: saving our allies. Simple as that!

Mighty Oaks ran the campaign in its early days with a ton of help from Sarah and her network of military friends, veterans, and advocates. Mighty Oaks functions because of generous supporters, and I did not want any of them to think I was using their donations to Mighty Oaks to fund our mission in Afghanistan. Sarah had similar concerns regarding her nonprofit work, so we decided to create a 501(c)(3) under the Save Our Allies name.

Anyone who has established a 501(c)(3) knows the legal steps and paperwork requirements take time. Members of the excellent staffs of Mighty Oaks and several of Sarah's close associates stepped up and created a nonprofit infrastructure in about two weeks. I can't begin to describe how proud I was to watch each of them selflessly step up to take action without question, complaint, or hesitation. They just did it.

Task Force 6:8

Andy—an old school Recon Marine with a very long résumé in the SOF and intelligence communities and who we referred to as Santa-6 over the following weeks because of his thick, graying beard—was already part of the team. Then I texted my good friend Tim Kennedy. Tim was a member of the US Army Special Forces, a Green Beret, a sniper, a top-ten UFC fighter, a well-known TV personality from History Channel's *Hunting Hitler* series and Discovery's *Hard to Kill*, and a guy just crazy enough to try anything once. But the main reason I reached out to Tim was because I trusted him as a close friend and a legit operator.

Beyond Tim's celebrity profile, he has extensive training and real-world experience in SOF ████ operations. He is not a has-been—he is still that guy and currently serves as a Special Forces Operations Sergeant (18Z) with the 20th Special Forces Group of the US Army National Guard, from whom Tim had to get approval to volunteer in the humanitarian efforts. I had talked with Tim about Aziz over the previous few months and knew he shared my heart and passion for our Afghan allies.

When Tim received my text, he was in Austin, Texas, with Nick Palmisciano, a West Point graduate, former Army Ranger officer, founder of Ranger Up clothing company, and highly intelligent guy who was running his own marketing agency, Diesel Jack Media. Tim, Nick, and I had been friends since 2010, when Tim and I both fought on Showtime's *Strikeforce* at the Toyota Center in Houston, Texas. As owner of Ranger Up, Nick was sponsoring us as military fighters, even hosting our after-fight party at Buffalo Wild Wings.

Tim replied that Sarah had texted Nick a few minutes earlier with the same request: Want to help us rescue Afghans? The four of us got on a call together, and Tim and Nick said they were in. We were four friends with a common and personal desire to get it right for Afghanistan when our own government was failing.

We quickly wound up with a twelve-person team. We also brought in Dave, a retired Army Special Forces officer and another West Point grad; Sean, a strong leader who was a career Army Special Forces officer and had been a

▮▮ contractor; "Seaspray," a Special Forces veteran and ▮▮ paramilitary officer; "Lee," a retired Army infantry paratrooper; Joe Robert, a brother Recon Marine who had been friends with Andy and me for about six years; and a few others whose identities must be protected.

My oldest son, Hunter, informed me he wanted to go too. As a father who will always want to protect his kids, I didn't want him to go.

Hunter had served in the Marines for almost seven years, through April 2021, as a member of the Marines' Air Naval Gunfire Liaison Company (ANGLICO). In 2019, he deployed to Afghanistan with the Georgian Liaison Team and embedded with the country of Georgia's military infantry as a forward observer to call in US air support. He also worked out of the base defense operations to control fire missions in support of the ANA. We are a Marines family. My other son, Hayden, is an active Marine as a crash fire rescue crewman, and my father served as an infantry Marine in Vietnam. Our three generations account for fifty-three years of consecutive service to the Marine Corps. The Robichaux family's military service began eighty years ago when my uncle fought in World War II.

From a military standpoint, I had no qualms with Hunter going. He was a great Marine, and I knew he could hold his own if anything went south on us. But from a mission standpoint, I feared that having a son with me would hamper my ability to focus.

I tried to talk Hunter out of going.

"You don't have to do this," I told him. "You have nothing to prove to me or anyone else."

"I have an obligation to go," he said, "because these guys I fought with that kept us safe and kept us alive, they have no help right now. So, I want to help them and their families. I'm booking our tickets."

Dang it!

He's his father's son, and I knew what was burning inside of him was the same fire that was in my heart.

(I learned later that Hunter also wanted to watch out for his dad, considering I was about to turn forty-six and hadn't been inside Afghanistan in fourteen years.)

Hunter was a man now, a Marine, and an Afghanistan War veteran. I couldn't rob him of an experience he would always remember. Nor did I want him to regret not being able to do the right thing when the right thing needed to be done.

Hunter emailed one of his colonels and informed him of our plan.

"I know we have about fifty Marines that were working with Afghans," Hunter wrote. "Can you get me a list of names of people we need to get out?"

The Afghans' names were in Hunter's inbox within five minutes. The colonel had already compiled a rescue list of interpreters.

In keeping with military tradition, and as a unique identifier among the other groups with similar aims, we came up with a name for our team: Task Force 6:8. The name was inspired by Isaiah 6:8: "And I heard the voice of the Lord saying, 'Whom shall I send, and who will go for us?' Then I said, 'Here I am! Send me'" (ESV).

Several of us had concluded this on our own and were shocked to find we all were led to the same verse for the mission. God was still orchestrating things. The context of that verse is the beginning of the prophet Isaiah's ministry. In a vision, Isaiah heard God asking who would serve as His messenger to the nation of Judah. Up to that point, Isaiah had felt unworthy because of his sin. But when Isaiah acknowledged his unworthiness and that his sins were atoned for, his desire to serve God led him to reply to the question with, "Here I am! Send me."

Now, we were answering a call of God. Send us.

A United Effort

Joe Robert knew the crown prince of the royal family in the UAE. Joe is a seasoned Recon Marine combat veteran with a hard personality matched by a mohawk and tattoos that extend onto his hands and neck. Yet, one layer below the surface, like many special operators, Joe is extremely intelligent and has an enormous heart for people. He and his family had a surprisingly deep global network, and his relationship with the crown prince proved more than convenient.

We needed a country where we could set up an operations command center, our JOC, and have support in moving evacuees. The UAE was the perfect location geographically.

Joe reached out to the crown prince and helped set up a call with the UAE's deputy ambassador to the United States. Sean, Andy, and I were part of the conversation. We also brought in Congresswoman Vicky Hartzler; Allen West, a retired Army lieutenant colonel and former member of the House of Representatives; and Rafael Cruz, father of US Senator Ted Cruz, to not only express their support for us and our plan but also ensure the UAE would receive proper credit for its role if, as we hoped, they decided to partner with us.

After we presented our plan, we received approval without hesitation. In addition to a place to set up our JOC in Abu Dhabi for overseeing operations, the royal family made an offer that floored us: two C-17 airplanes for flights in and out of Kabul, pilots, use of an airstrip, and access to the humanitarian center in Abu Dhabi for housing refugees. The humanitarian center included every resource we could think of—or, in my case, not think of needing: food, lodging, doctors, medicine, teachers, and processing centers for immigration to other countries, to name a few. The UAE's generosity was incredible. Just one round-trip flight would cost the UAE at least $800,000, and the crown prince knew the number of flights would be many.

I've been asked often why the UAE was so generous. The UAE has historically opposed radical Islamic terrorism, and with its location in that region, I don't think the UAE wanted to pick a fight with the Taliban. In working with them, I also saw their compassion for the people inside of Afghanistan, regardless of whether they were Emiratis. The UAE had the resources to help, and its leaders felt compelled to do the right thing.

As awareness of our effort increased, an official representative of Albania contacted us and offered hotels and resorts as temporary holding spots for anyone we evacuated. Mexico and Ethiopia told us we could bring evacuees there. We also heard from Canada, Pakistan, Greece, Qatar, Russia, and Ukraine.

At home, we were blown away by the generosity of individuals as they learned about Save Our Allies.

In just over one month's time, we raised $2 million. Half of that amount came from five donations. The other half came from about five thousand individual donations.

We were full-on nose-to-the-grindstone, working long days, and seeing the outpouring of support—from individuals, organizations, and nations—was so encouraging in those early days. Politics didn't matter. Nationalities didn't matter. Religious beliefs didn't matter.

One example comes from a Jewish organization that contacted us before we had set up Save Our Allies to receive donations. Their donation would have to go through Mighty Oaks, but when they looked into us more and learned that we are a Christian nonprofit, the organization said that as a Jewish organization, it would not be able to send money to us.

We replied, "You realize we're rescuing Muslims, right?"

"Oh, yes," was the reply.

Laughter followed, and then, "No problem."

That group donated specifically to cover the cost of flights for evacuations.

So, a Jewish organization wound up donating about $1.6 million through a Christian nonprofit to help rescue Muslims! How awesome is that?

On an individual level, I was hearing from people who appeared to derive pleasure from commenting negatively on my social media accounts in the past when I've (frequently) promoted conservative values. But they were sending supportive messages of our efforts—and donations.

Publicly, I made no secret of my disappointment in our government's actions. I was dumbfounded by some of our political leaders' decisions on both sides of the aisle and, frankly, embarrassed that we abandoned Americans, our allies, and vulnerable people groups. I was heartbroken knowing they had risked their lives for my country and our military service members and now had their lives endangered. I was carrying the frustrations expressed to me by numerous members of our military who, like me, knew what awaited at the end of the path our country's leaders had chosen.

A very large, and growing, group of people simply wanted to help other people in their time of need.

And the need was staggering.

Even before all the legal boxes were checked on Save Our Allies becoming a nonprofit, Sarah set up a JOC in DC, and I made media appearances to put the word out that we were looking for American citizens, interpreters and their families, and vulnerable groups including Christians, women's shelters, and orphans in need of rescue. I posted on my social media accounts, with some of my update videos on Instagram drawing more than three hundred thousand views. Tim posted on Instagram, where he has over a million followers.

Over the first ten days of going public with our campaign, we received more than twenty-two thousand requests for evacuations.

Seven

★

Chaos at the Airport

AFTER KABUL FELL, THE FIRST PART OF OUR TASK FORCE 6:8 team headed overseas to set up a JOC in the UAE. I remained in the United States for a few more days to continue working on operations logistics for when the team arrived in Afghanistan and to work with Sarah setting up a system for the flood of requests coming to us.

Sarah worked the DC angles, taking responsibility for coordinating with government officials to ensure we did everything legally. We were carrying out a moral cause—rescuing our fellow man—and knew we had to precisely follow the law with the Office of Foreign Assets Control (OFAC) under the US Treasury as well as coordinate with the Joint Chiefs and the US State Department, which to me felt as though it was working against us every step of the way. Sarah brilliantly navigated those relationships and kept us out of trouble and operational.

Sarah and I were calling members of Congress, communicating what we were doing and collecting their support. Interestingly, some of the requests pouring in to us came from congressional offices and officials from government agencies who felt they were prevented from being able to bring their priority allies out. Parts of our government were looking to NGOs—and not just ours—for help.

As of Friday, August 20, we estimated one hundred thousand Americans and allies needed to be brought out of Afghanistan. The next day, Sean, Seaspray, and Dave flew from Abu Dhabi into Kabul as our first boots on the ground. Tim and Nick would later fly into the UAE with Hunter and me, and then Tim and Nick would travel on to Afghanistan. Once we had everyone in place, Andy, Joe, Hunter, and I, along with others, would work operations and coordinate rescues from the JOC in Abu Dhabi. Sean, Seaspray, and Tim would be our three-man rescue team working outside the airport while Dave remained inside HKIA to coordinate with the military. Nick would spend one day helping Dave and then return to the UAE to work with us.

With the rest of us inbound, Sean, Seaspray, and Dave went to work immediately upon arrival. They described the airport scene as total chaos. Thousands were gathered outside the gates hoping to be allowed in. August is the last month of summer there, and temperatures were reaching into the midnineties—plenty hot, especially for the elderly in the crowd and children. Those who brought bottled water with them were already running out. People were fainting or lying on the ground out of exhaustion. Some were trampled.

Moms were kissing their babies goodbye—most likely for good—and handing them off to be crowd-surfed toward the gate in hopes that a member of our military would mercifully take the baby inside the airport. The news reports showing video of our service members pulling babies over the walls yanked at the hearts of Americans back home. What wasn't shown was babies also being tossed over the walls. Behind those walls were coils of concertina wire about five feet high and twenty feet deep. Concertina wire barriers are crimped so they cannot be separated once put together. Whether it is used for a military purpose, in prisons, or as protection against animals, concertina wire is designed to keep people and animals from attempting to cross it and trap anyone or anything that tries anyway. When Joe made a later trip into HKIA, he saw six dead babies who had bled out lying in that jumble of wire.

Early on, Sean was moving to make rescues outside the gate. He was within inches of two people when they dropped to the ground, shot dead by the

Taliban. Sean stepped over their bodies and kept moving forward through the crowd to get to his mark.

A buddy of mine told me of the Taliban beheading two young Afghan men and holding up their heads to taunt US Marines, knowing the Marines could only stand there and watch.

Chaos didn't seem like a strong enough word to describe the area surrounding the airport.

The preceding Monday was the day that produced the video images many of us will carry for the rest of our lives: Afghans, in the hundreds, sprinting down HKIA's runway as a US Air Force C-17 cargo plane accelerates for takeoff; people trying to find any part of the plane they can clutch on to, some grabbing hold of the front landing gear; and then, as the plane ascends a few hundred feet, those men falling from the plane and to their deaths.

If the world didn't already know how desperate Afghans were to escape the Taliban, it learned that day.

The US military had to restore order at the airport.

Commercial flights were temporarily halted as our military took over air-traffic control. When we asked the military why commercial flights had been shut down, they told us that so many NGOs wanted to fly planes in for evacuees that coordinating flights had grown beyond its capability under its current responsibilities. Dave suggested that if we were provided a dedicated ramp for access to HKIA's one runway, he would serve as an air traffic controller and coordinate all the commercial and NGO flights so that one at a time could come in, load up with evacuees, and take off. The military accepted the offer, and Dave handled all nonmilitary aircraft coming into and leaving the airport.

The Baggage Handler in the Pilot's Seat

The State Department had issued a shelter-in-place warning to discourage Americans from risking a trip to the airport. Many waited in terror, not knowing their government was days from leaving them stranded and at the mercy of the Taliban.

It was in that environment that Aziz was updating me on each failed attempt to get his family to the airport and through one of the gates that would secure them a flight to freedom. As bad as the airport scene sounded through media reports, it was much worse based on what I was learning from Sean and from my WhatsApp calls with Aziz as I tried to help him navigate a path to the airport. Sometimes he had to whisper to avoid detection, and at others he had to yell over screams and gunfire.

The Taliban had strengthened its control of Kabul, including checkpoints leading to all airport entrances. Although the Taliban had told our government and our media that it would allow safe passage to the airport for those with proper documentation, they were whipping and beating people and taking their passports and documents that proved their right to leave.

The Taliban had established checkpoints around the airport, and our Marines were responsible for security of the airport itself. But Aziz and others were telling me of another layer in some places between the military and the Taliban—"Zero-Zeroes," or Unit 00 resistance fighters from within the Afghan intelligence agency, the National Directorate of Security. Aziz's family faced having to make it past three rings of security to get inside the airport.

To disperse the crowds to avoid another nightmare civilian overrun of the airport and runway, US helicopters were flying overhead and launching smoke grenades, and Marines, Taliban, and Zero-Zeroes were firing into the air. The Taliban were beating people with the stocks of their guns. They imposed a nighttime curfew in Kabul and, during the day, fired shots at Afghans protesting in the streets.

Despite continued reports that the Taliban had agreed to allow evacuations, they were blocking access to the airport. Still, thousands of Afghans crowded the airport gates, and the numbers seemed to be growing each day.

British and German troops were flying in and out of HKIA by helicopter to rescue their citizens, and our US service members could only watch in confusion and frustration, wondering why they were not allowed to do the same for their fellow countrymen.

The reason was that the military was not calling the shots. We were in a noncombatant evacuation operation (NEO), which is the removal of civilian noncombatants and nonessential personnel from a dangerous location. NEOs are traditionally the responsibility of the Department of Defense, but the White House had handed that oversight in Afghanistan to the State Department. Yes, to the diplomats, the negotiators. The military was considered too emotionally attached to the Afghans because of their twenty-year relationship.

Placing the State Department in charge of an NEO is like taking an airline baggage handler and placing them in the pilot's seat of a Boeing 777. They're going to crash the plane because they aren't trained to fly it. Our State Department was in charge of an operation that was neither its job nor within its expertise. They did what they knew to do; in essence, the airport had become an embassy in that it was a place to be processed for departure from Afghanistan—if someone could get into the airport.

For Americans, unlike citizens of other countries, the airport was not a place of rescue. The military, which was trained to rescue people in NEOs, was working for the State Department, and now its job was perimeter security, the same as being embassy security guards. The military could defend the perimeters, but by State Department order they could not get anyone to safety or intervene in any way to help Americans outside the airport perimeter. Not even if they witnessed Americans being harmed. (One exception I am aware of came when three CH-47 Chinook helicopters flew less than the length of about two football fields to a hotel and evacuated 169 Americans because crowds had made walking to the airport unsafe.)

We had connected with some amazing special operations team members inside the airport who were prepared at a moment's notice to perform rescue operations. They wanted to help Americans and our allies and offered to do so. They were furious that they had to stay inside the airport while watching other nations' militaries make repeated runs outside the perimeter to pick up their citizens. We also had individuals from a cross-section of government agencies contact us saying they were willing to help us outside the scope of their duties.

From my military experience, I knew the risk the special operators were taking by offering to help—and I'm not talking about just risking their lives. The military mindset when given an order you don't agree with is to suck it up and carry out your duties with the same degree of professionalism as when you agree with an order. If caught, they could be court-martialed and probably kicked out of the military and/or sent to jail. And these were guys with enough service time and status that they would be putting their careers on the line if they helped us, other NGOs, or trapped Americans. In a time when everything felt so wrong, it was an encouragement to see people's willingness to simply do the right thing.

An argument could be made regarding the lawfulness of the orders and whether the special operators were obligated to follow orders if human life was at risk. That was not up to me to decide. I'm all about military structure and order, but I was moved by their courage and am proud such men exist. These guys, as well as the government employees, were telling us they would rather suffer the consequences if caught than live the rest of their lives with the guilt of doing nothing while innocent people died. And this wasn't only about saving American lives. They wanted to rescue the innocent Afghans, too, because being part of the human race meant more in that moment than anyone's nationality. They were guided by the same simple principle that led us to create Task Force 6:8—they were compelled to answer the call to do the right thing.

Even if Only One

One of the biggest problems we were all dealing with was that the orders coming down from the White House had placed the wrong people in charge of the airport. The diplomats had negotiated that the Taliban would provide outer security for the airport while saying the airport was ours. In military tactical terms, we did not "own" the airport. We had given the Taliban the outer perimeter of an enclosed area, and in battlefield strategy, whoever controls the outer perimeter—especially access to and from the inner perimeter—controls the ground space. That's why when a military wants to capture a space, it surrounds that space and chokes it out.

By owning the space around HKIA, the Taliban controlled the airport and access to it. They weren't going to try to take the airport by choking our military out. Why would they? Patience was their best strategy, and the Taliban is good at the long game. Our military was given a clear line that it could not pass going out from the airport. We placed that noose around ourselves. All the Taliban had to do was block access and bide their time, especially since we had given them a date. That's exactly what they did.

No matter what the State Department claimed about the Taliban agreeing to allow safe passage to the airport, Americans couldn't get there safely. The State Department essentially acknowledged that when it released its shelter-in-place order. In practice, we gave the Taliban permission to check our people's documents and determine whether to let them through their checkpoints.

Around the time our Afghanistan team was arriving in Kabul, the messaging from the White House began including the phrase "who wants to leave," as in the government would evacuate every American who wants to leave Afghanistan. Just a few days earlier, senior administration officials had told Senate staff during a private meeting that ten to fifteen thousand of our citizens were still in the country. Just days before on Wednesday, August 18, President Biden had made a commitment that every American and ally who wanted to evacuate Afghanistan would be evacuated, even if that meant missing his August 31 deadline for full withdrawal. "We're going to do everything in our power to get all Americans out and our allies out," he promised.[1]

President Biden knew he had placed himself in a position not to keep his word to the American people, at the cost of our citizens and allies, so he and the State Department entered into negotiations with the Taliban to extend our withdrawal deadline. The Taliban said no.[2] If it wasn't clear before, the world now knew that the Taliban, a terrorist organization, was calling the shots on the withdrawal, not the United States or President Biden. We had already given away negotiating power. We never should have asked the Taliban for an extension. We only needed to tell them, "We will leave when we are done with our evacuation. End of discussion. If your Taliban soldiers get in the way or harm any American, we will respond with force, and it will delay our departure. Stand down, stand aside, because we will evacuate every single American and ally we choose to before we go."

I didn't receive the memo that America had changed its policy of never, under any terms, negotiating with terrorists. This is why. Yet now we were little more than a week until the deadline, and we obviously would be leaving Americans and allies behind. That's not what we do as Americans.

We have demonstrated this throughout our history. When fifty-two Americans were held hostage in Iran back in 1979, it took 444 days to bring them home, but we did. More recently, we showed the lengths we would go to rescue one American. Army soldier Bowe Bergdahl was captured by the Taliban in 2009 after deserting his post. He was held for five years until the Obama administration exchanged five high-ranking Taliban members held at Guantanamo Bay for him. Bergdahl was tried by court-martial and pleaded guilty to desertion and misbehavior before the enemy. We paid a high price to bring him home. Our military employed significant resources to try to find Bergdahl when he went missing. Those involved in the search said soldiers died because they were trying to locate him. But they went looking for him because Bergdahl was one of ours. I would have searched for him, too, despite how I felt about him as a deserter. We don't decide not to do whatever it requires to rescue someone because we think he did something stupid. Our military will use all its might and strength, and we'll scorch the earth if necessary, even sacrifice life, to rescue one of our own. We don't leave Americans in danger behind enemy lines. But in Afghanistan, there was no doubt we would.

The addition of "who wants to leave" communicated a lack of under-standing of the situations faced by many who wanted to leave. Even before the first shelter-in-place order, Taliban checkpoints proved an effective deter-rent for trying to reach the airport. It was common knowledge they were confiscating passports and beating people who they publicly claimed were being permitted to pass through those checkpoints. One of our team mem-bers witnessed the Taliban brutalize a man caught with an ID card stating he worked with the US military. The Taliban held the man down, melted the ID card into his chest, chopped off both of his arms, placed a noose around his neck, and dragged him down the street behind a vehicle—in front of his adolescent son. The man was one of our allies. Although he was not an American citizen, any American trapped in Kabul hearing that story would be reasonably hesitant to attempt passing through a Taliban checkpoint carrying a US passport.

Also, many of those still in Afghanistan had spouses, children, and other loved ones they did not want to leave behind. Getting a family to the airport instead of just one person presented far more challenges.

The phrase "who wants to leave" also misrepresented why many Americans were in Afghanistan in the first place.

We had been in Afghanistan for twenty years. After we removed the Taliban from power, Americans led the rebuilding of the country. Afghanistan had much infrastructure that needed to be built, and that meant numerous construction contractors going there to work.

Many of our citizens were also there for humanitarian purposes. We had medical workers in hospitals and clinics. We had educators in schools and missionaries representing many religions. Christians were willing to take risks by waiting to leave because they believed God had called them there. Aid workers would stay in the country as long as possible out of their compassion for the Afghans. They were not there for financial motivations. They were there because they cared. Those were the types of people who were still in the country. And it's also worth remembering the stunning rapidity with which the Taliban took over the country in contrast to what US officials had projected, by a matter of months. Our president had previously said no American would be left behind, and then the State Department issued its shelter-in-place directive. That's a textbook case of having the proverbial rug pulled out from under you.

One of the most fundamental responsibilities of the US government is to protect its citizens at home and abroad. The number of American citizens who needed to be rescued was much discussed during the withdrawal, and rightfully so.

Three weeks after the withdrawal ended, Senator Jim Inhofe of Oklahoma, the ranking member of the Senate Armed Services Committee, said in a speech on the Senate floor that the Biden administration had knowingly left Americans behind, and he accused Secretary of State Antony Blinken of being dishonest regarding the number of American citizens still in Afghanistan.

"Early in the evacuation," Inhofe said, "Secretary of State Blinken said that there were perhaps 10,000 or 15,000 American citizens in Afghanistan. Our men and women in uniform, working tirelessly and effectively with our diplomats under incredibly difficult circumstances, managed to evacuate about 6,000 of our citizens. Now, according to my math, that means that between 4,000 to 9,000 Americans were left behind. But Secretary Blinken says that there were only 100, and that the rest preferred to stay in Afghanistan. . . . So, that is more than bad math; it is a lie."[3]

The White House also used Secretary Blinken's numbers.

Which number was real? Was it one hundred? Four thousand? Nine thousand? More? Truthfully, the correct answer does not matter as long as there is at least one, because one American's life is worth every bit of diplomatic leverage and the full force of US military power to bring that American home. Our government had the duty to rescue each and every citizen and bring them home safely—whatever that required.

Eight

★

Saving Aziz

I HAVE FLOWN IN AND OUT OF HKIA MANY TIMES. THE international airport is on the northeast edge of Kabul, and densely populated residential areas are to its south, west, and northwest. But there also is a bit of a buffer of open terrain around much of the airport. The Taliban could not stand shoulder to shoulder to secure the airport perimeter because it was far too large a land mass. Imagine the major airport where you live; you could cover access points and observe open areas, but the perimeter would be porous.

Sean, Seaspray, and Dave were at HKIA while Tim, Nick, Hunter, and I were preparing to leave home for the UAE. Sean and Seaspray's first assignment outside the wire was reconnaissance work to identify the Taliban checkpoints and setting up ratlines, or escape routes, leading into the airport.

The best way to locate the checkpoints was good old-fashioned walking and looking. With the Taliban executing people trying to escape, the worst scenario would be for our rescue team to start smuggling people through an airport gate believed to be secure and then have the group compromised by the Taliban.

The Taliban owned home-field advantage. The spots for sneaking into the airport were either known by the Taliban or would become known to others—militaries, civilians, groups like ours trying to help civilians escape—and they established checkpoints all around those places. That set up a cat-and-mouse game for circumventing those checkpoints that required studying geographical features for building routes to bypass them.

But clearing the Taliban line was only the first step. There still were the Zero-Zeroes working outside the airport, the crowds, and then, finally, US military stationed at the gates.

Meanwhile, Sarah and a group of volunteers in DC were processing the rescue requests pouring in through a triage system of categories we established: US citizens, SIVs with documents, SIVs without documents, P-1 visas (citizens with certain threats of persecution), P-2 visas (employees of the US government and contractors not meeting SIV qualifications), Christians, vulnerable women, and orphans.

We were receiving rescue requests from people outside those categories whose desperate pleas were heartbreaking. Sadly, we had to stick to our triage process.

One such request came from a man who told of his uncle who had given up hope of getting out of Kabul with his five daughters. Faced with the near certainty that his daughters would be subjected to a life of sex slavery to the Taliban, he shot and killed his five daughters and then killed himself. The man who told us that story begged us to save his life. But he did not qualify for our list and probably wouldn't make any other NGO's lists either. Every day we had to confront the horrible feeling that we were essentially playing God by picking who to save and who not to save.

The lists compiled by Sarah's team were sent to me, and I coordinated their rescues through our on-the-ground team led by Andy in Abu Dhabi.

All our linkups were in Kabul. We told anyone outside of the city to come to Kabul to meet us. For linkups within two miles of the airport, our rescue team worked on foot. Outside of two miles, they used vehicles. I worked tirelessly to find a means for using helicopters in rescues, but when I finally did, complications with the potential source of helicopters forced us to abandon that idea.

Over forty US-trained Afghan military pilots had flown their planes and helicopters into other countries to escape the Taliban. The Taliban demanded the pilots return to Kabul with their equipment if they left Afghanistan. We tried to convince some of the pilots to fly the planes and helicopters to a country that would give us access to the equipment, but that didn't pan out either. Every door that closed only pushed us to be innovative and resourceful as time was still ticking. It had, however, become clear that our rescues would be limited to ground-based movements, although we continuously tried a variety of out-of-the-box options. Ours was an orthodox operation that required unorthodox means.

We communicated through WhatsApp initially and then later shifted to the Signal app when we learned WhatsApp had become compromised. We established a protocol that had to be followed to the letter to ensure someone couldn't fake us out and infiltrate our process. I'll stop just shy of saying our system was foolproof, but if anyone beat the system, we have no idea how they duped us.

First, on the day of the rescue, we required the person to send us a vetted proof-of-life photo, such as them holding their documents and an item displaying that day's date, like a newspaper. After that step, we provided an exact time and pickup location. At the pickup, we employed far and near recognition symbols. The far symbol was a picture or an image on a phone that the person would display to our team from a distance. We constantly changed the symbol. Once our guys could see the far symbol, they were comfortable getting close to the person (or group). Then, the person was required to state a password, which we also kept changing. Next, the person would have to provide the paperwork and all supporting documents required to leave the country, such as a passport, a national identification card (Tazkira), a letter of reference, a military contract for services provided, awards, and proof of service. If our guys could match the face of the person to the face on the documents, they would take them through one of the ratlines to HKIA.

Our first rescue was a young woman named Narna.

When the rescue requests first started coming in, I was helping process emails and sending them to Sarah to be categorized.

One caught my attention because of what turned out to be a mistake in the subject line, which I believe was God's divine providence. The subject line read "American u student needs help," so I opened it immediately thinking we had an American in danger. The man who sent the email had intended to type "American University student" because he was seeking help for an Afghan attending American University of Afghanistan.

When I read the email, I knew we had to move quickly.

Narna was twenty-one and worked in President Ghani's office, which to the Taliban meant she was Westernized. The Taliban had snapped a picture of her and texted her the photo with a message saying they knew who she was and would rape and kill her. They already had grabbed Narna once and beat her up pretty bad, but she'd managed to escape.

The man's email said Narna was hiding and told us how to contact her. I sent Andy her number and a quick message stating the urgency to find her right then. Andy called Narna through WhatsApp, and she told him she was hiding under a stairwell inside a multistory office building about a hundred yards outside the airport. She said the Taliban was in the building searching for her.

No one on our team was positioned to get to that building immediately, so Andy called inside HKIA to a small group of what we can only call good-hearted US special operations members who had informed us they would have preferred being outside the airport rescuing people. The guys sneaked outside the wire and hurried to the building. In the process of clearing each floor, they spotted Narna being dragged out back by the Taliban, moments away from being raped and killed. All I can say about the meeting between the two groups is that the Taliban clearly recognized the Americans wanted Narna, and they released her. Our courageous, unsung heroes escorted Narna inside the airport, and she became the first person for whom we coordinated passage into the safety of HKIA.

Our team's first day of rescue operations resulted in 150 people flying to Abu Dhabi.

One More Try

I had to do a lot of convincing for Aziz to make his eighth and, he said, final attempt to reach the airport. Because of the Taliban checkpoints, the Zero-Zeroes' presence, and the massive crowds, the first seven attempts had failed. Aziz had lost hope.

On the seventh, at night, I had coordinated with Sean, who was waiting for the family at a gate when Aziz called and said they were turning around. He was covering seven-year-old Mashkorallah's ears while talking to me, and I heard shooting in the background. I'd heard shooting on a previous call too.

"I just need you to go for it," I pleaded with Aziz. With Bashir and his Taliban thugs looking for Aziz and his family, I believed it was more dangerous for them to turn back. But Aziz also knew the accounts of what the Taliban were doing around the airport. They were beating people. They were shooting them to death. They were cutting off heads and arms. They were tying a rope around people's necks and dragging them behind cars through the streets.

"I can't, brother," he said. "Mashkorallah is scared. I've got to go back."

Aziz didn't believe his children, especially his youngest ones, could take hearing more of the gunshots the Taliban were firing into the air to scare people or worse. They'd witnessed the Taliban strike people to the ground with the stocks of their guns. They'd been pushed and shoved within the thousands of people outside the airport. Afghans had heard on the news, Aziz said, that the United States said it would accept anyone who had worked for its government and also anyone who had not worked for them. As Aziz put it, the people thought the door to paradise was open, and being the closest to the airport gates was their only chance to get in.

Aziz made attempts during night and day, by different routes and entrances, but nothing he had tried worked. After the seventh attempt, he said the airport was too dangerous to try again, so he would try to come up with a way to leave by foot into a bordering country.

I didn't think Aziz could make it out of Kabul alive. He had already been turned back at two Taliban checkpoints, and I didn't like his chances of avoiding being recognized a third time or being found by Bashir. I asked him to go to HKIA one more time.

"I trust you, brother," he said. "I'll try one more time."

For this final attempt, I sent Aziz a pinned location via Google Maps, and I assured him we would again have someone there waiting for his family.

Aziz arranged for a friend to pick up him and his family in the morning and drive them to an open area near the airport. Aziz's daughters started crying during the drive, anticipating repeats of the violent scenes that had played out in front of them and shut down the previous attempts.

When the friend parked the car, Aziz told his family to remain inside. He wasn't willing to put their lives in danger until he could first determine that someone was waiting at the pickup spot. But Aziz couldn't make it to the spot we had arranged, and he messaged me to tell me he was at the north gate, on the opposite side of the airport.

I messaged Sean and got on a call with him to tell him Aziz was in a different location and that Aziz would not be able to stay there long enough for Sean to get to him. Sean called inside HKIA to the senior enlisted leader of a US ████ Special Operations ████ team, Master Sergeant "HY," who had been helping us. Sean briefed him on Aziz, and HY agreed to go to the north gate to meet Aziz and bring him inside.

We linked everyone up through WhatsApp, and HY told Aziz that he and his team were on their way to meet him outside the airport.

The area was relatively calm, allowing Aziz to wait there. He spotted a small pararescue team exit the north gate across the road from where he was standing about fifty yards away. But they were wearing body armor and helmets, and Aziz couldn't recognize if it was HY's group. Aziz climbed onto a large, shaky rock, and while trying not to shift his weight too much and flip the rock over, he yelled, "HY! HY! This is Aziz!" But HY didn't hear Aziz. Then Aziz saw a teammate next to HY get his attention and point toward Aziz.

By now, Aziz had raised the awareness of Zero-Zeroes and Marines securing the gate. The Zero-Zeroes pushed Aziz, trying to get him to back away from the area. A few Marines came over and shooed Aziz away. Aziz tried to show them his documents. "I'm your ally," he told them. "I worked for you guys. I put my life on the line. I worked for Chad. Do you know Chad Robichaux?"

"I don't know him," one of the Marines said. "Get away."

Someone from one of the groups fired a warning shot in Aziz's direction.

Then HY yelled across the street, "That's my guy! Don't shoot at him!"

"Come over here!" HY shouted to Aziz.

Aziz sprinted across the road and embraced HY.

"My family's over there," Aziz said, pointing to the open area in the distance. "I was not able to bring them. It was very difficult to get here. I need your help. Please tell these Marines and these other guys to let me bring my family."

The warning shot had brought attention to that area. More Zero-Zeroes came rushing in, increasing their number into the hundreds. Some were firing into the air to spread out the crowd that had been stirred up by the first shot. Some were striking people with their guns to try to control them.

Amid the growing commotion, HY got the attention of a Zero-Zero commander. HY and his team had already gone against orders by coming outside the airport gate.

"Look, this is my guy," HY told him. "He needs to bring his family here. Walk with him and escort him all the way through your guys. He and his family are very important."

"Okay," the commander responded. "I'll walk him to that area where our guys are, but I'm not going to walk with him over to where the Taliban are."

The commander and Aziz started walking toward his friend's car.

"Please don't leave," Aziz told the commander. "These other guys do not know me. They won't let me come back."

The commander accompanied Aziz as far as he said he would, which was about twenty yards from where Aziz's family waited.

Aziz feared that if he walked away to get his family, the commander would leave. Aziz called his friend and asked him to drive the car to a spot across the street from Aziz and the commander. The friend followed Aziz's instructions, and Aziz was able to walk to the car while nervously keeping an eye on the commander to make sure he didn't leave. Aziz realized that bringing his family together across the street would get the Taliban's attention; a family moving together obviously would be trying to get into the airport. Instead, one by one, attempting to blend in with the surroundings so he would not be recognized, Aziz slowly walked all seven members of his family from the car to the commander.

The commander then returned with Aziz and his family to where Aziz had met up with HY. HY and the ███████ team came back outside the gate in an armored Hilux pickup truck, and they hurriedly loaded the family and the two bags they carried with them—containing all the possessions they were hoping to leave their home country with—inside the pickup and sped back inside the gate.

When the Hilux had cleared the last of the various checkpoints maintained by ally militaries, HY snapped a selfie with Aziz and sent the photo to us. That's when I learned that my brother and his family had finally—finally!—made it safely into HKIA.

Aziz was exhausted, mentally and physically, when at 9:30 a.m. they stepped into a line of people inching toward the airport terminal.

While the family waited in line, Aziz messaged me, tired and emotional but overwhelmed with joy and expressing his appreciation. I was emotional and tired, too, and I couldn't find the words to say other than I was so happy he and the family were safe and that I couldn't wait to see him soon in Abu Dhabi.

The final hurdle Aziz needed to clear was confirming his identity against the US biometric database of Afghans who had assisted coalition forces. Once that box was checked, we informed Aziz that he and his family were now safe. All they needed to do was stay in line for a flight out.

Around 2:30 p.m., after five hours in line, they were within a few minutes of reaching the end of the line for boarding a US Air Force flight to Qatar and then on to the United States. Thankfully, one of our planes from Abu Dhabi landed at that time, and Sean called Aziz and told him we had a different flight for his family. The Marines supervising the group didn't want to let Aziz and his family out of line because people were trying to move ahead in the line by breaking in front of others. Sean told the Marines that Aziz's family was with him, and he walked them over to where they could get on our flight returning to Abu Dhabi.

Not surprisingly for Aziz, we had to make him get on the plane. Because he knew his family was safe, he didn't want to be among the first groups to leave Afghanistan.

"I need to stay with you guys to help you here," he said.

Typical Aziz. But we were not having it. He had done enough for us in the past. Now was our time to do this for him.

At some point back home that day, amid communicating with our Afghanistan team and vetting emails to send along to Sarah, I paused just long enough to reflect on our first day's success. We had rescued 150 people, including Aziz and his family.

Those of us from the military community tend to be confident people. And for good reason. We receive the best military training in the world, and we learn to plan not only for our objective but for all kinds of obstacles that could pop up at any point during an operation. We don't say, "We have a plan," until we are certain it's a solid one. I was sure our plans would work, and I had zero doubts about the ability and integrity of every member of the team we had assembled. But, honestly, I experienced moments while reading emails and seeing the lists of names we'd vetted to rescue when I just couldn't know if we would be successful. This was different from anything any of us had ever done, with so many variables completely out of our control.

Afghanistan had spiraled out of control more rapidly than expected even by those of us who had predicted the country's fall into the Taliban's hands. And who could know if our own military would be ordered to shut us down at any moment? We were racing against a clock to save as many people as we could in an unknown time frame that was nearing its end—soon.

But we had rescued 150 people in one day. They would live freely again.

We actually did it! I thought, and then I got right back to work. At least ten thousand Americans and ninety thousand allies were looking for a way out. We had just begun.

Nine

$=== \star ===$

Every Second Matters

COORDINATING RESCUES FROM HOME IN REAL TIME MADE me want to be part of the rescues on the ground.

From 150 rescues the first day, we jumped to 800 the second and set a daily goal of 1,000. On the third day, Monday, August 23, Tim, Nick, Hunter, and I departed for the UAE.

After coordinating our efforts from my home outside of Houston, Texas, it was clear my best contribution was in that role. Our team was so experienced that each of us could have capably filled any role, whether overseeing operations from outside Afghanistan, coordinating from inside HKIA, garnering support, or going outside the wire for rescues. My work was similar to my work in the ▮▮▮▮▮▮ task force in that we were planning unconventional operations from scratch and making it happen.

Also, working in our UAE command center would allow me to continue accepting media interviews to raise awareness and the much-needed financial support for our rescue operations. Still, I wanted to try to get into Afghanistan before the deadline arrived.

I looked forward to going to Abu Dhabi to better sync with the guys in Afghanistan because the difference in time zones between Kabul and the UAE was only thirty minutes. I also could be 100 percent focused on the job. In Abu Dhabi I would be able to focus on our mission better, and already we were realizing that every second of a break we took could mean lives lost.

Kathy had had plenty of time to get used to both Hunter and me going to the Middle East. She knew I was headed to the UAE, although going into Afghanistan remained a possibility. But she figured the most I would do there was help load people onto a plane and fly back out to Abu Dhabi without leaving the Kabul airport.

From the standpoint of executing the mission, I had no concerns, and she seemed okay as well. But I did have a physical concern.

Even though I had been working twenty hours a day in my home office, I made time to get a workout in at Carlson Gracie Houston, my Brazilian jujitsu team. I was stressed out—I believe every member of the team was—from knowing that tens of thousands of people were so close to an unlucky crossing of paths with the Taliban that would cost them their lives. I wasn't sleeping, eating, or hydrating enough, and I needed to get into the gym and unplug. Stepping onto those mats and grappling is my stress-reliever because when I'm immersed in my work, jujitsu helps me unwind and be present, even for a moment. I'm able to make better use of my time after working up a good sweat and clearing my mind.

I went to our school and met up with one of my students, Kevin, a tough MMA fighter I had been training since he was a kid. We were going at it hard when I went for a takedown. But Kevin had his head to my side. If I completed the throw, I probably would have spiked him on his head, so I modified the throw to protect him. That placed me in an awkward position, and as I started the throw, I felt a pop in my groin. I rolled around on the mat, moaning in pain. I had to be helped to the side and needed an hour there to recover. Then I needed to be helped to my feet and could barely climb into my pickup to drive home.

The next morning, I underwent an MRI scan and sent the images to a surgeon friend who worked for a professional sports team. The adductor longus muscle had completely detached from the pubic bone.

"You need emergency surgery," he told me.

I told him I was leaving for overseas in a few days and that I had three important questions.

"Can I hurt it worse?" I asked.

"No," he said. "It's detached from the bone, so it's as injured as it can be."

"If I have to run from something—hypothetically—will it fail me?"

"No," he answered, "because you have four other muscles there still working."

My last question was, "Is it going to hurt bad?"

"Yes," he said. "But you'll be fine."

"Okay," I told him. "That's all I needed to know."

I chose to hold off on the surgery. (I still haven't had that surgery.)

My primary concern was not being a liability to the others if the ground team wound up in a run-for-our-lives scenario. I could deal with the pain, and I declined a prescription for the pain because I needed to keep my mind clear. As a lifelong athlete, I believe if you're going to function with an injury, it's best to feel the pain rather than numb it. Pain is a gauge that tells you where your boundaries are so you don't make the injury worse. I needed to feel the pain as a tool for knowing my limitations. If the surgeon had told me I would be more limited, that would have made for a more difficult decision because I would not want to put my teammates in danger on account of my injury.

I upgraded to business class for the flight to UAE so I could lie back and take pressure off my groin and hips. But my groin still hurt to the point that I asked a flight attendant for a bag of ice—which I kept covered with a blanket, because who wants to be seen on a plane with an ice bag on your groin?

My second concern was mental. Even though I was going to the UAE to coordinate operations from there, I still believed that I would be back in Afghanistan at some point. I hadn't been in a war zone since my PTSD diagnosis. Being in the UAE command center would pose no physical safety concerns. And if I did go into Afghanistan, it was looking like I'd just be flying into and right back out of HKIA. The airport wasn't a safe and secure environment for the average person, but it would have been compared to my experiences. It wasn't like being in the remote environments I had worked in many times before.

But I still carried memories of my last flight into the UAE, fourteen years earlier, when I was on the run after escaping my captors and fighting for my life. I had been isolated in the Persian Gulf for those four days with a nervous breakdown and debilitating panic attacks. The location was just up the coast from Abu Dhabi, and I had never forgotten the dusty smell there. I hadn't come across that smell anywhere else. And Middle Eastern perfumes sold in the duty-free space of the airports also carried distinct aromas. Would the outdoor dust layer or even the airport perfumes trigger something within me that would make me fall apart again?

Or would my name pop up when passing through customs because of my previous travel to Pakistan? I was probably wanted there by ISI. I checked before leaving, and the UAE did not have an extradition treaty with Pakistan. But my first time back, I couldn't assume anything.

On the flight over, I prayed, *God, I am going to go do this because You have put the burden on my heart to help these people. I need You to protect me and keep me free from any physiological effects in my mind and body and keep me safe from any enemies new or old.*

A peace came over me not only for the rest of the flight but for my full stay in Abu Dhabi.

As Hunter and I exited the plane, I told him we needed to split up before entering customs.

"If they hem me up," I told him, "do not come to me or get engaged. Get out of the airport and call Andy."

Hunter went ahead of me. When I approached the customs agent, he looked at my passport, stamped it, and motioned me through. "Welcome to Dubai."

I walked out of customs, and Hunter was right there waiting for his old man.

We traveled an hour and a half to Abu Dhabi, where we were able to grab about an hour of sleep. We woke up and met with Tim, Nick, and Joe to plan out our initial integration into the operations there. A flight was about to return to HKIA in an hour or two, and since Joe and Andy needed me in the JOC, it was just going to be Tim and Nick on that flight out to join

Sean, Seaspray, and Dave. Saying goodbye to Tim and Nick as they departed brought back an old feeling I hadn't experienced in years—that last look you give someone before they go, and you know there is a real chance you will never see them again. I couldn't help but consider they were getting on that plane because I had asked them to, and they trusted me. Yet I had no control of the environment they were stepping into. Tim is usually loud, joking, and always having fun. But his tone was serious. This was real, and our lives would all be in danger along with those we were there to save—Aziz and many others whom we didn't even know. I looked at Tim and Nick one more time as we walked in opposite directions, and I prayed to myself, *God, be with them, blind the enemy, miraculously protect them, and give us success to save these people.*

When Tim and Nick arrived, Sean and Seaspray were on their way outside the wire. Within fifteen minutes of stepping off the plane, Tim had changed clothes and our three-man team was leaving the airport for the first time together. That night they set up eight ratlines, including ones that passed through the sewage ditches that received attention on news reports. The gate the UN accessed had been sealed shut when the UN left the country. Tim cut off a couple of locks and bent and cut some rebar so the gate could be pried open just enough to move people through. The team also made cutouts in fences to pass people through.

Operation Chivalrous Knight

I was back in the UAE, but on a new mission.

From the moment I stepped into our Abu Dhabi command center, the UAE government was beyond incredible in its generosity, hospitality, and professionalism. But in our first meeting, UAE officials—mainly their team of lawyers—pressured us to get the people we were bringing into the humanitarian center transported out to other countries.

"They are your responsibility," they told us. "You have ten days to get them out of here."

I didn't like the pressure, but I understood where the lawyers were coming from. The UAE, which allowed us to bring 4,100 evacuees into the country, already had taken steps through its immigration policies to prevent being overrun with refugees after the withdrawal announcement. Our numbers had ramped up in a hurry, and we were already closing in on the UAE's limit. Plus, I knew the lawyers and officials were the ones responsible for making good on the royal family's offer to bring evacuees there. I knew what it was like to have a boss say, "Yeah, we'll do that," and then leave it up to me to figure out how.

I couldn't offer a solution. We were private citizens of the United States, an NGO trying to help. The State Department held the power to allow evacuees to move to safe harbors in the United States.

Fortunately, Ken Isaacs of Samaritan's Purse stepped in with an offer I immediately accepted. Ken was a vice president overseeing the international relief projects of Samaritan's Purse, and I received an unexpected call from him. He wanted to confirm that we were moving a thousand people a day, as he had heard. When I said that total was correct, Ken asked if he could fly in to see how we were managing those numbers. Samaritan's Purse, led by Franklin Graham, the son of the great evangelist Billy Graham, is one of the most impactful organizations in the world and one I have admired and hoped to partner with at Mighty Oaks. Receiving a call from Ken was exciting and encouraging. I had not met Ken but knew he was one of the world's best leaders at dealing with humanitarian crises. Ken came to Abu Dhabi and spent a day with us, and when I told him I needed to step away for a meeting and described the pressure we were receiving, Ken said, "Do you mind if I go in there with you?"

I couldn't show Ken the way to the boardroom fast enough.

Ken's presence in that meeting changed the environment. They knew who he was and what he knew. Ken kindly but firmly told the UAE officials, "These guys are not responsible for relocating these people—the US State Department is. They have no authority over the State Department, so put pressure on the State Department."

Before Ken returned home, he also made a sizable financial contribution on behalf of his organization and started making arrangements for places where we could send evacuees. His reputation and that of Samaritan's Purse didn't disappoint.

Unexpectedly hearing from Ken and benefiting from his expertise and help is just one story of how people and offers were popping up seemingly out of nowhere. God consistently brought people and resources that made it possible for us to rescue as many people as we did.

Overall, the UAE didn't just roll out a red carpet for us—they rolled out a red carpet lined with gold. Our command center was set up in the five-star Armed Forces Officers Club and Hotel, with a view of the majestic Sheikh Zayed Grand Mosque. They catered meals for us and provided two luxurious conference rooms to work in.

The entrance to the military building where we worked had "The Chivalrous Knights" written in Arabic at its entrance. Based on that entrance, they named our joint rescue mission Operation Chivalrous Knight.

The UAE committed its best resources to helping us. Not that we had time to enjoy any of the luxuries, but they did everything they could to enable us to be completely mission focused. In fact, our rescue work was so urgent that I didn't have time to go see Aziz's family at the nearby humanitarian center until my third day there. Working in a fluid, constantly evolving situation meant sleep was a luxury. Both the team in Abu Dhabi and our ground team in Kabul were sleeping maybe an hour a day, but the team in Kabul slept in anything but luxury. (Seaspray, who's a fit, muscular dude, lost thirty-seven pounds in his ten days running rescues.) No one on either team wanted to sleep, because getting away for even one hour brought feelings of guilt, knowing that every second we were away equated to lives lost. I struggled to understand how anyone could be sleeping anywhere in the world knowing what was happening there. I specifically wondered how the world's so-called leaders could sleep, how they could witness such atrocities and not act. Edmund Burke once said, "The only thing necessary for the triumph of evil is that good men do nothing." From the looks of it, the world needed some more good men.

We met twice a day with UAE officials: usually a representative of the royal family, four military leaders who I equated to generals based on the stars on their uniforms, the interior minister, and about twenty lawyers. In one of our first meetings, I did something I never thought I would need to do in my lifetime: I apologized for our country. I'm a proud American and as patriotic a man as you could hope to find. But I know what's right is right. The UAE was helping us rescue Americans when our government appeared to show little interest in doing so, and they deserved an apology and a thank-you for their generous support.

While I handled rescue rosters, Andy and Joe coordinated with Dave to get flights from the UAE to Kabul scheduled and manifested. Andy and Joe also coordinated with the UAE pilots and their two C-17s and the commercial planes and crews provided by Mercury One and The Nazarene Fund, which were founded by longtime friend Glenn Beck. Among the heroes and people who stepped up during these evacuations, Glenn and his team were all in from day one. Glenn and another good friend, Dave Barton, called me in the UAE and extended no-questions-asked support for flights out of Kabul. Rudy Atallah led their efforts as COO of The Nazarene Fund. Rudy was a retired USAF lieutenant colonel from the special operations and intelligence community with extensive real-world experience in rescue operations and in combating terrorism and human trafficking. The group he led went above and beyond in providing twenty-seven flights for us that cost them over $20 million. These people are the real deal and were incredibly committed to saving those vulnerable in Afghanistan.

Our work rooms in the Officers Club were round with marble walls. It was like working inside a cylinder. In our main work area, our desks faced toward the center, where we could stand and easily address everyone in the room. We tracked the groups needing rescue via large sheets of white, self-stick, flip-chart paper placed on the wall. Dozens of sheets circled the room. We built rescue plans for each person or group represented by a sheet, communicated the plans to the team on the ground, and connected those needing to be rescued with our team members. It seems a little crazy on the surface that we were creating these intricate, secret rescue operations and then employing everyday apps such as WhatsApp, Signal, and Google Earth. But we had to use what the people we were rescuing could access. At one point, WhatsApp became compromised by Pakistan's ISI, which was giving the Taliban access to calls. We switched to Signal, although security was a concern with that app as well.

That is the challenge—and thrill—of special operations work. We had a saying in recon related to combat dive operations and military freefall jumps: "Plan your dive and dive your plan." Because not everything goes as planned, part of the plans needed to include contingencies. We would plan, plan, plan for every conceivable contingency, but we worked in fluid environments and wound up making and executing decisions on the fly. That seems to be how real life works too.

For the most part, however, our rescue team was able to stick with the plans we created. Even though I coordinated rescues through Andy and wanted to make the best decisions possible for our team on the ground, Sean, Tim, and Seaspray were free to revise as needed. They were among the highest-skilled operators on the planet, and they knew how to adjust on the fly and get the job done. And their lives were just as at risk as the people they were rescuing every step of the way.

Ten

---★---

Safety First—There
and for Back Home

MOST OF OUR OPERATIONS OCCURRED UNDER THE COVER of darkness, although we were able to move larger groups during the day by bringing them to the airport on buses.

As with everyone we brought into the airport, we made triple certain anyone we allowed onto a bus was properly vetted. The US government has been accused of evacuating the lucky souls who were in HKIA, regardless of status. While that may ring true, our efforts were handled with military precision. Our government was adamant that we weren't sticking just anyone on a plane and flying them out of the country. Most NGOs working alongside us did due diligence in vetting people as well.

We knew exactly who we were getting out because of the triage process that Sarah oversaw from the States. We compiled manifests that included the reason for evacuating each person, and Sarah ensured every manifest went to the Joint Chiefs of Staff for review and action. We also worked closely with congressional offices and multiple federal agencies since our efforts were legitimate in action and access—a feat no one else was able to accomplish.

We required every American citizen to show us their passport or green card. Afghans had to show us their passport, Tazkira, or other identifying documents. Because groups were contacting us with names of people they needed to get out, we also had that extra layer of vetting. Women who were part of a vulnerable group, for example, could not bring a man with them. Ministry housing groups and orphanages were required to vouch for the identity of each person they brought to us.

The only individuals I recall working with were SIV cases, and at minimum they had to show us their submitted application. All our flights were to lily pad locations, or third-party countries where the evacuees also would receive additional vetting from the US State Department. We were not flying anyone directly to the United States.

I believe it's important that people understand, first, how stringent the vetting requirements were for NGOs like us and, second, how rigidly we worked to meet all the requirements. In the first few months after the withdrawal, we saw incidents of Afghan refugees committing crimes on US military bases while being housed for processing, and my concern is that the NGOs will be blamed for bringing those people into the country. In my opinion, the US government should be held responsible for their entry.

The government and military were not following anywhere near the same vetting processes as the NGOs. I've had the privilege of talking face-to-face with Afghan refugees now in the United States, including some who were evacuated on our flights and others on the Department of Defense flights. They tell me how individuals they recognized as Taliban and ISIS members were boarding Department of Defense flights at HKIA. They saw prisoners who were released from the Bagram prison waiting among the crowds outside the airport gates. Especially in the initial days after Kabul fell, when the White House needed positive numbers to report, the military would crack open a gate and let a specific number of people through. Those who managed to secure a spot at the front of the gates were the strongest and fittest—basically, the men. They were getting in ahead of women, children, families, passport holders, and SIVs. Those getting through—like the Taliban and ISIS members—were only getting a pat down before being brought straight to America.

The day before I left for the UAE, the White House announced that almost twenty-eight thousand people had been evacuated over the previous eight days. I believe those numbers were accurate because the military and government were getting a lot of people out in a hurry. The problem was who they were bringing (including those who would commit criminal acts upon their arrival) and who they weren't bringing (American citizens, SIVs, the vulnerable). They weren't vetting evacuees like the NGOs were. In fact, Save Our Allies chose to pull out of our resettlement work at one military base and called the state police after the rape of a young boy was being covered up by the military leadership there. That incident is under review by the Senate Permanent Subcommittee on Investigations.

As important as vetting was, the process NGOs were required to follow was so stringent that it hampered our efforts. Our Afghanistan evacuation effort at Save Our Allies ended up being the second largest next to the US military, but I say it was the largest evacuation of vetted individuals.

One day, we worked over seven hours to move a group of buses carrying 334 people inside the wire at the HKIA perimeter. On board were American citizens, orphans, women, Christians, and families of pilots of evacuation flights. The ground team had vetted and searched every one of them and had arranged to bring them to an entry point at HKIA. When the buses arrived, a US military officer told Sean he needed to see the manifest containing the names of each person on those buses. We had multiple government agencies secretly sending us names of their people they wanted us to rescue because bureaucracy had tied the agencies' hands. Some of the people on the buses were from those government agencies, and Sean needed to protect the identity of those individuals and their agencies.

The officer recognized Tim and made a comment about the rescue work becoming "the Tim Kennedy Show" because of Tim's large public profile.

Tim remained professional and ignored the remark. Sean told the officer that he could tell him generally who was on the buses but that he could not hand over the list with every name. The officer said that if Sean didn't show him the list, he would not allow the bus inside the airport. Sean proposed having everyone on the buses step outside and show the required documents, which we had already vetted.

"If they're good, they go back on the bus," Sean offered. "If they're bad, you can do whatever you want with them."

"These people need to leave," the officer said. "They need to go to the checkpoint and do it the right way."

That checkpoint was a Taliban checkpoint, and his "right way" was obtaining approval from the Taliban.

An argument ensued and the officer, who owned the final authority, won. He kicked the group of 334 outside the safety of HKIA and back beyond the Taliban checkpoint. The group included 27 American blue-passport holders and over 100 orphan children. We were unable to reassemble that group for another attempt. Who knows what happened to the American citizens that one of our own military leaders forced back to the Taliban? The incident was immediately reported, the officer was relieved of his post, and the incident is currently under review by the Senate Permanent Subcommittee on Investigations.

On another occasion, another officer stopped one of our groups from entering HKIA because he said we were creating too much work for the military inside the airport. Granted, the military was providing MREs and water for the people we brought inside because we didn't have the manpower to provide care. We were getting out over one thousand people a day, with a one-day turnaround from when we brought them in until they were on a plane and leaving. We had our own staging area at HKIA, and we typically had about two hundred people at a time waiting for our next flight. Sometimes there were more, but we set a threshold for when we would have to pause rescues to get caught up, and we never had to pause.

The military had its hands full, though, with the large numbers they were allowing into the airport. They had their own holding area, like a hangar, designed to accommodate fifteen thousand people. At one point, there were twenty thousand people in that holding area with no restroom facilities.

Although the hangar was covered, it was hot like an oven inside. The military was doing the best it could to distribute MREs and water to everyone under their care. But people died in that holding area because of the hot weather. Of course, people were dying outside the airport too because of the conditions. The Biden administration placed our military in a situation that was too difficult for it to efficiently handle with the numbers and resources they were given. I am in no way speaking down on our men and women in uniform. They bravely did everything they could. Many did beyond what they were allowed to, and all were frustrated with their limitations. They were set up for failure from the onset of the withdrawal.

"Peace to You"

One amazing aspect of our rescues is that we did not lose a single person or team member. That's unbelievable considering the circumstances in which our guys worked. But there were close calls. We received public criticism, especially toward Tim and me on social media, from people who said we would get ourselves killed and that they hoped we would die because we were doing something we had no business doing. Everyone understood the risks. We were not naive about what could happen to us. This wasn't our first rodeo. Yet we all decided the work and the people were worth the risk.

One rescue involved a family with three young children. The father informed us he was receiving text messages from the Taliban calling the family by name and saying the Taliban knew the linkup location we had arranged. We changed the location twice trying to throw off the Taliban.

When Tim arrived at the linkup spot, he saw the family and also heard military-aged men talking with one another. The father passed our identification protocols, and Tim started leading the family toward the airport. The Taliban followed for what turned into a twenty-minute foot pursuit with Tim carrying the youngest, a girl about three years old, the entire time.

Standard operating procedure included setting up four routes back to the airport following the military's PACE acronym: primary, alternate, contingency, and emergency. Complicating matters before the gates started being shut down was that we couldn't just show up at any gate and get in. We had to establish routes ending at a specific gate where we had arranged entry with help from a member of the military. Or, especially in our later rescues, to a secret spot where we had created our own means for entry.

Tim started the family along his primary route, but once he realized they were being tailed, he had to start using back streets and alleys even though the Taliban knew Kabul much better than he did. Tim wound up working his way to his alternate and then his contingency routes until arriving at a parking lot adjacent to HKIA. There, Tim and the family hopped over a wall and weaved their way through abandoned cars and buses until they reached an accessible gate and entered the airport.

Tim also had several face-to-face encounters with the Taliban.

One came when the team was going outside the airport to scout a location and identify Taliban checkpoints. Not all checkpoints were stationary, because the Taliban also used roaming guards. This spot was near the airport's main entrance. Once the commercial side of the airport had been shut down, leaving only the military side open, the Abbey Gate, which received so much attention in the media, became the de facto main entrance. Abbey Gate was just to the east of the old main entrance.

Tim sneaked his way through the terminal and out through an employee entrance, low crawling around concertina wire. Even though the terminal was closed, the Taliban had set up several checkpoints there, we speculated for no other reason than as a show of force for news media photos and videos.

Tim was making his way around a corner when he walked into a three-man Taliban patrol rounding the same corner from the opposite direction.

"Salaam Alaikum," Tim said to them, the common "Peace to you" greeting there. That was the only appropriate thing to say because not acknowledging them would have created more suspicion. Our training taught us that when you're somewhere you aren't supposed to be, don't just act like you belong there, act like you own the place.

The Taliban did not respond.

Tim was holding an AK-47. The three bad guys were carrying rifles.

The way Tim told the story, the two sides stood there for a moment evaluating the situation and each other. He was poised on the balls of his feet to shoot or move if they made a move at him.

In Tim's favor, he had long hair and a beard and looked more like a dirty homeless man than military. Also in his favor, he had switched his AK-47 from the safe to fire position. He thought the Taliban's rifles were still on safety, although he couldn't be sure.

Tim believed he could have killed all three of them before one could get him, and based on watching him at the range, I'm confident he could have. But that would have attracted the attention of the other Taliban nearby. Also, fighting the Taliban was no longer our fight. Our mission was to save people.

Tim continued to look at the guys, wondering whether "the juice was worth the squeeze." Apparently, neither side wanted any juice that day. He backed away slowly, and the three Taliban backed away slowly until they could safely resume their duties of the Taliban patrolling the area and Tim identifying Taliban locations.

He found them.

Eleven

━━━ ★ ━━━

Leaving Afghanistan

AFTER A FEW DAYS IN ABU DHABI, I FINALLY WAS ABLE TO SEE Aziz and his family.

All the refugees were placed into a fourteen-day quarantine in Abu Dhabi because of the coronavirus pandemic. Let's just say I knew a few people who made it possible for me to visit them despite the quarantine.

Following our emotional reunion in Aziz's room, we were taken into a common area. I hadn't seen my brother in fourteen years, but almost as soon as we took our seats next to each other on a couch, we were right into telling old stories like we had been apart for only fifteen minutes.

I was most surprised by the sorrow Aziz expressed as he talked about leaving his home and how he felt like he had lost his country. Although I knew he loved Afghanistan and had seen him fight for its freedom, I didn't think leaving would hurt so deeply.

Aziz's parents, two brothers, and sister were still in Afghanistan. His escape meant he likely would never see them again. As much as Aziz had the safety of his wife and kids in mind while getting out, he was equally torn about leaving his family behind. One of his brothers had also worked with us on the ███████ task force. Bashir knew Aziz's brother, and he would be a Taliban target for sure. His parents and sister could have been too because of Aziz's high profile.

But Aziz's dad insisted that Aziz take his family out of the country.

"I've lived my life," Aziz's dad told him. "Me and your mom are older. You need to go get your family safe and live your life."

Not surprising for Aziz, he stepped up to become a leader in the humanitarian center. I jokingly gave him the title of Humanitarian City President.

The humanitarian center was an incredible facility located about a ten-minute drive from our JOC at the Armed Forces Officers Club and Hotel. The UAE government ran the center well.

The setup was like a series of apartment complexes, so families had their own places to stay, which included cable television. When our team noticed the kids were getting bored, we told the UAE government, and they built a playground on the level of what we would expect in a nice neighborhood in the United States.

The humanitarian center even had doctors and nurses on-site, which became an unexpected necessity when up to three babies a day were being born. We assumed we had thought of everything! The evacuees also were arriving sick from dehydration or with broken bones, cuts, and bruises suffered from being stampeded or getting caught up in the concertina wire at the airport.

The center also provided dental care. And the meals were great.

Aziz used the word *chaos* to describe the humanitarian center when he first arrived. Of course, after all his attempts to make it into the Kabul airport, chaos was relative. The initial chaos at the center was understandable. By the time of my reunion with Aziz, we had brought in more than 5,000 evacuees. We were past the UAE government's original limit of 4,100—the pressure from the lawyers was getting even thicker—and we figured thousands more were coming. When one lawyer asked about the numbers being over, I joked and said we were "overachievers." He didn't laugh. The rapid fall of Afghanistan didn't allow time for preplanning and trying to stay within limits. We had to get the people safe and then figure out how to make things work.

Aziz stepped in and organized a system in which each building and each floor within those buildings had its own leader.

"All those leaders report to me," he said.

President Aziz had set up an organizational structure and chain of command. He made sure that everyone had food, water, diapers, and whatever other basic living supplies they needed since most had left Afghanistan with nothing more than they could stuff into a backpack.

He never stopped surprising me, and watching him lead reminded me why he was so special. Although Aziz was sharp and organized, what made him a strong leader was that he was all about other people—always serving and leading.

Aziz had thought he could help us by staying behind inside HKIA. It turned out that we needed him more in the UAE, and he proved essential there. He had a humanitarian center full of his fellow countrymen he could care for, all of whom were there because of him.

In what was like a full-circle moment for me, Aziz and Hunter worked together there. Even though "Uncle Aziz" had offered to watch out for Hunter during his yearlong deployment to Afghanistan, they didn't meet each other until the humanitarian center.

Hunter had spent our first few days in the UAE helping set up the JOC. When the JOC was in good working order, Hunter, Lee, and two others in the humanitarian center inventoried the refugees. Hunter started the process and then Aziz joined him. I wished I could have spared a few minutes to sit back in the shadows and watch Hunter and Aziz work together. I had told Hunter countless stories about Aziz, and he was finally able to see in action the Aziz I had described.

Hunter and I had a conversation about the fact that because the US military had been in Afghanistan for twenty years, we were a father and a son who had served in the same war and now were working together in the fallout of that same war. How many fathers and sons could share that experience? I hope not many.

I was glad Hunter had persisted until I agreed to let him come. He was the youngest member of our team, but he jumped right in and asked, "What do I need to do?" Of course, we took advantage of his youthfulness whenever computer and other tech issues came up. The young guy solved all us old folks' tech problems.

As the one overseeing our evacuation operations, I knew Hunter made our team stronger. As his father, I could see he was in the middle of a once-in-a-lifetime experience that will forever influence him.

I also was able to see how hard a worker Hunter was. Not that I had doubts, but it was good to witness firsthand how he was willing to do anything he could to meet whatever need arose. Being inside the humanitarian center was nothing like being in Afghanistan. But it was a secured facility, and Hunter was locked inside with thousands of Afghans who didn't speak English and were frustrated by the uncertainty they faced and scared for loved ones still in their home country. I was super proud of Hunter. What he and the humanitarian center team did required courage. Sure, it was different work than the ground team's in Kabul, but it was courageous work nonetheless.

And I hope Hunter enjoyed seeing a different side of his old man. He's always known me to be an intensely driven, full-charge, mission-focused guy. This was the first time he was able to see me in an environment where that part of my personality worked best.

Working alongside Hunter was a once-in-a-lifetime experience for me, too, and I am thankful for it.

A Father and His Son

After that trip to the humanitarian center to reunite with Aziz, I returned almost every day to see him and the family, even if for only a few minutes. My schedule had little margin for leaving the JOC, but that first visit had convinced me I needed to go when I could. The humanitarian center brought me back to the reason our team was split between Afghanistan, the UAE, and Washington, DC, working essentially around the clock.

The pace had been so frantic since we arrived. I was taking short breaks for quick media interviews and social media updates, but other than grabbing about an hour of sleep, we were completely mission focused. All the numbers we'd been chasing—this group of twenty we needed to move from here, that group of thirty from over there, the group of a hundred that couldn't get to the airport on their own—and all the white sheets of paper we'd stuck to the wall suddenly became people's faces for me because of the humanitarian center.

There, I could stand and watch families embracing each other when they discovered they had both made it out safely. I could see looks of relief. I could see crying. I could see people staring off into the distance like they were in shock. I could see the loneliness. All the different stories that had brought this collection of people into the humanitarian center were being told through all the different expressions and emotions.

I was tired. I was consumed by the burden of knowing people's lives depended on us. I was, well, a lot of things. And I needed to see the people we had rescued to that point to keep me operating at maximum efficiency for all the others we were going to rescue.

On one of my visits, Hunter told me about talking with a mother and daughter who had made it onto a plane without their husband and father. They broke down in tears as they described how worried they were about who they had left behind. It didn't require a stretch to imagine how in Afghanistan this mother and daughter had feared being raped or killed and had made it out alive. Yet they also had family members and friends still there, still facing the same threats that, for some reason, they had been more fortunate than their loved ones to escape.

We walked the grounds and observed children running around, their hair all messy but with smiles on their faces because they were safe. Some were too young to understand the concept of safety, but even if they could not articulate the sense of evil and the fear they had left behind in Afghanistan, they could run around here freely because of what they sensed in their parents. Even though all these families were in an unfamiliar place, they were in a better place.

"This is freaking real," Hunter said to me. "These people, and these little girls, would have had no chance of living if they were under Taliban rule."

I also saw a boy about thirteen years of age sitting by himself, looking off into nowhere. I took Aziz with me to interpret, and we asked the boy if he was okay. He straightened up his posture and put a grown-up expression on his face. He said he was fine. I knew better.

As Aziz and I talked with the boy, he opened up and told us that as he and his parents and sisters were trying to make it to the HKIA gate, the Taliban started shooting in their direction. As the family started to scramble, the boy got out ahead of his family. He turned and looked back to wait for them. His dad shouted to him, "Just go inside! We will meet you inside!"

The boy made it through a gate, but he couldn't find his family inside the airport. He was boarded onto a plane bound for Abu Dhabi alone, still hoping to locate his family.

I asked how I could help, and he said he wanted to call his parents. I handed him my cell phone, and he called both of his parents' numbers. Neither answered. He left both voice mails saying he was safe in Abu Dhabi and asking where they were.

For the next few days, each time my phone rang, I reached for it hoping the call was coming from one of his parents. They never returned the boy's call. I pray they are alive and will someday reunite.

As Hunter was helping inventory the evacuees, he came across another boy about fifteen years old with a similar story. He introduced him to the boy Aziz and I had talked with, and they became friends. Every time I saw those two boys, they were together, sometimes smiling and playing, at other times clearly processing the likelihood that they would never see their families again.

I carried the images and stories back with me every time I returned to our JOC, where the cliché description "roller coaster of emotions" fit.

Think of a football game: two teams play for four quarters, and at the end, the team with the most points is the winner and the other is the loser. Now, imagine if a football game were played in such a way that every single play determined a winner and a loser. In a typical NFL game, the teams run about 125 plays combined. That would be 125 wins and losses crammed into three hours.

That's how our work felt.

We were in constant communication with our Kabul ground team, updating our lists, peeling white pages off the wall. The emotionally difficult part to handle was running off long streaks of victories and then receiving a report like the one that a scheduled linkup with a group of two hundred orphans didn't happen, with no explanation. We had to scratch the group off our list—not just two hundred names but two hundred kids' faces like the ones playing freely in the humanitarian center. The same situation occurred with another group of three hundred orphans. There was no linkup at the designated time and location, and no explanation. Then, of course, there's no suppressing your imagination of what might be happening to the orphans in that very moment if the Taliban had reached them before we did. Each time we lost a group, I had to peel the white paper off the wall and toss it in the trash. I had to move on to the thousands still on the way. We had to move on. There was no time to grieve.

I read the frantic emails pleading for our help.

"The Taliban is threatening me. . ."

"My wife is going to be killed. . ."

"They beat me. . ."

"They killed my son. . ."

"I am afraid for what will happen to my children. . ."

That's why we slept only an hour a night. That's why we ate at our desks as we worked. Every second, an Afghan somewhere in their country was desperately looking to their phone, hoping we would call or respond to their message or email. And it wasn't a game to see who wins and loses. Even with every little victory, the big picture of Afghanistan was a loss.

As Hunter said, it was freaking real.

Shut Down

Late afternoon on Thursday, August 26, at 17:50 local time a VBIED suicide bombing outside Abbey Gate killed 13 US service members and approximately 170 Afghans hoping to be allowed inside the airport. Eighteen other

US military members along with well over another 200 Afghan civilians were severely wounded.

When I received word in Abu Dhabi of the attack, my first thought was, *Are our guys okay?*

We immediately got in touch with Tim. At the time of the explosion, our ground team had just completed loading evacuees onto a C-17 about a mile away. They had been at Abbey Gate minutes earlier. The cargo ramp was still down on the plane when they heard the blast and a dust plume rose from that area. They could not tell what had happened, but they knew it was bad. They closed the ramp right away and sent the flight off.

As the reports came in detailing the number of US service members killed, I got angry. Our military had not experienced that much loss of life at once in Afghanistan since ten years earlier, when thirty Americans lost their lives. The Taliban had shot down their helicopter with an RPG in the Tangi Valley, known as Extortion 17. Seventeen of those killed were Navy SEALs, most of whom were from my old ▮▮▮▮▮ task force. Some of the families of those killed in combat claimed the deaths were the result of President Obama's ROEs. Of course, President Biden was vice president then, so it is hard not to tie the two incidents together and put responsibility on the highest levels of White House leadership, the commander in chief.

Although the suicide bombing at Abbey Gate turned out to be the responsibility of ISIS-K, attempts back home to try to separate ISIS-K from the Taliban were nothing but attempts to avoid accountability. The Taliban and ISIS-K may be enemies at times, vying for power and territorial control, but they both subscribe to the doctrine of Sharia, and despite any minor theological differences between the brands they follow, they agree on Sharia's compulsion toward jihad and its obligation to hate "infidels." Thus, the Taliban didn't try to run ISIS-K away from the airport. They allowed ISIS-K to be there. And, of course, we soon learned that the suicide bomber had been released by the Taliban from the prison at Bagram a few days earlier. To anyone who cared to see the truth, the Taliban and ISIS-K were one and the same during this attack.

The deaths at the airport did not need to happen. Our team had talked about how such a bombing was inevitable because of how the State Department had postured our military in such a static perimeter with no standoff. The Biden administration placed our troops in a situation where they could not defend themselves. Our young military heroes died because of bad decision-making.

Thirteen service members dying in one blast made it obvious too many of our troops were too close together outside of cover. Especially considering the previous reports of legitimate suicide bomb threats made in that area, consolidating Marines and sailors in such a crowded location was poor planning. It wasn't the service members' fault—they were following orders. As could be seen from the images of our troops taking babies being passed through the crowd and then caring for those babies inside HKIA, our troops were doing what they could to save lives. In the process, thirteen Americans lost their lives, two hundred others died, and many were injured. The deaths and injuries were tragic and avoidable.

Stories from the bombing quickly came to our team.

A Marine buddy of Hunter's was at Abbey Gate and watched one of his teammates die. A Recon Marine who attended a unit event I spoke at a few months earlier died. HY, our pararescue friend who grabbed Aziz, told of coming into contact with one of those killed. He had spotted this young Navy Fleet Marine Force corpsman, who was serving with the Marines and had earned the nickname "Doc," with about fifteen to twenty kids gathered around him. None of the kids had adults with them. A few were clinging to him. HY walked over to Doc, who said, "I can't leave them."

HY asked how long he had been with the kids.

"I don't know—all day," he answered.

"Let's bring some in," HY said.

They loaded some of the kids into a car and drove them inside to a small triage center. HY then drove the corpsman back to where the rest of the kids were and dropped him off. About fifteen minutes later, the explosion occurred.

HY was able to inform the young man's mother that the last thing her son did was sit with the scared kids outside Abbey Gate and comfort them. What an absolute hero to mankind.

Call me cynical, but my first thought was that the White House would respond to its embarrassment by retaliating and blowing up an empty building or taking out some random people just to show they did something. In politics, bad news needs to be quickly replaced by good news, and the military often is a tool employed in the politics of foreign policy to create the good news.

In response to the attacks, President Biden made a statement that included these words to the attackers: "Know this. We will not forgive. We will not forget. We will hunt you down and make you pay."[1]

Oh, no, I thought. *We're going to blow up something.*

A day later, a drone strike in eastern Afghanistan took out what were called two "high-profile" members of the group responsible for the suicide bombing, although specifics about the identities of these high-profile targets were noticeably absent. President Biden said that strike would not be the last.

It wasn't. Unfortunately.

Two days before the withdrawal deadline, another drone strike near the Kabul airport killed suspected suicide bombers in a vehicle packed with explosives, according to the Pentagon. An Afghan government official claimed the bomb struck a home and killed civilians. The Pentagon later admitted the strike had mistakenly killed a worker with a US humanitarian organization and nine other civilians, including seven children. Two of the children were two-year-old girls. No one was held criminally responsible for the mistake. The unanswered question is, Who identified that target? A bombing like that is either a target someone lasers to guide the bomb or identifies by providing a coordinated grid. Or someone had to provide our military information that the NGO worker was a target. If the latter was the case, who provided the information we acted on wrongly? Were the Taliban now serving as forward observers for us? These are more important questions added to the ever-growing list, all without answers or accountability at the time or since then. In fact, with respect to the suicide bombing, the Pentagon briefed the findings of their investigation to the media on February 4, 2022. US Army Brigadier General Lance Curtis, who led the investigation, said,

Based on our investigation at the tactical level, this was not preventable and the leaders on the ground followed the proper measures, and any time there was an imminent threat warning they followed the proper procedures: they lowered their profile, they sought cover, and at times, they even ceased operations at the gate.[2]

The general is correct that the young service members on the ground at the tactical level did everything they could to protect and evacuate the innocent given the spot they were put in. That spot included being told to coordinate with the Taliban for security at the ground level, necessitating that some of these young service members communicate with those terrorists over their own cell phones—an unimaginable personal security debacle.

Thus, for true accountability, what is needed is a full investigation of the military and civilian leadership's actions at the strategic and operational level, where we clearly failed.

Those who put our young men and women in this horrible position at the Kabul airport are the same people who decided to close and evacuate Bagram Air Base. I wondered how many of them watched on big-screen monitors as flatbed trucks poured across the border of Pakistan to seize and transport billions of dollars of American military weapons and hardware from Bagram back across the border. I wondered why none of them chose to intervene.

Losing our service members made me more determined to do our job. We talked with our team on the ground to ask if they believed the environment had become too dangerous to work in. Despite warnings of a possible follow-on attack, each said he wanted to continue the operation.

The bombing's aftermath created more challenges for us with a week remaining until the United States' self-imposed deadline.

Two more gates were welded shut, further restricting entry points. We also received word from inside the airport that military leadership had started pulling troops back from security responsibilities, which was one way we were able to bring people inside. The new challenges meant a mix of overt and covert operations was no longer an option for us at HKIA. The additional security threat forced us to work covertly and avoid all major gates.

Our troops were being instructed to clean the airport for handover to the Taliban. Yes, our military, in its final week in Afghanistan, amid the desperation to evacuate American citizens, SIVs, and vulnerable groups, was spending its time cleaning urinals. The service members talking to us were describing how low morale had become among the troops and that some were refusing orders to clean the airport. I, and everyone privy to this knowledge, was livid and disgusted. If anyone knows what an upper decker is, be assured the Marines left more than one for a final shot at the incoming Taliban. (Look it up for a laugh.)

I learned later from Marine leadership that not only were the Marines and soldiers at the airport put in an impossible position but also the Marine Security Guard tasked with guarding the US embassy in Kabul.

Looking back to April 13, 2021, when President Biden announced the September 11 withdrawal date, the State Department called on all embassy personnel who could work remotely to move back to the United States. Still, at that time among the security personnel was an assumption that the Afghan military could and would defend Kabul and that the embassy would stay open into the foreseeable future, requiring that Marines be there to guard it. However, those assumptions began to be challenged after the Taliban conducted a complex bomb and gunman attack on the home of the minister of defense on August 4. Over the course of the following week, the Marines were informed that they would need to be ready to leave by the end of the month. Then, during the weekend of August 13–15, they were told it would be two weeks, then seventy-two hours, then forty-eight hours, then twenty-four hours, and eventually less than twelve hours.

This rapidly shrinking timeline caused the Marines to have to quickly begin destroying classified materials, personally identifiable information, and other items that the Taliban could use for propaganda. By the time they were forced to do this, the US mail service had been shut down, so the Marines were unable to ship any of the embassy's property or any of their own personal property home. They were initially told they could pack two checked bags and a carry-on and that everything else needed to be destroyed. This resulted in the young service members burning nearly everything they owned, including their dress blue uniforms, more than one hundred American flags, and even a framed picture of the beloved Marine hero Lieutenant General Chesty Puller.

All the while, as they took to the task of destroying their own property and coveted artifacts from a piece of what was sovereign American soil, these Marines were receiving frantic calls from around the world—mostly from other service members who were desperately trying to help other American citizens and loved ones (including spouses) trapped in Afghanistan and, in some cases, being hunted by the Taliban. These Marines could do nothing other than pass on the information to the State Department.

As the heartbreak and shame turned to anger, the Marines took to destroying anything and everything that could provide any comfort to the Taliban. Unlike those at the airport cleaning toilets for the Taliban, these Marines broke toilets to pieces. All of this came to an end on Sunday afternoon, August 15, when they were called on to lower and present the American flag to Ambassador Ross Wilson, who served as chargé d'affaires. By the end of that day, the embassy had officially closed, and the Marines left on helicopters. All had to leave behind their checked bags, and some even had their carry-on bags (containing the only possessions they had left) tossed from the helicopters to save weight, forcing them to evacuate the country without a single thing more than the civilian clothes on their bodies. This wasn't Saigon all over again; this was worse.

I had not realized it at the time, but the State Department had closed the back valve on us—intentionally, I now believe.

OFAC rules allowed NGOs like us to carry out our humanitarian work in Afghanistan. We were registered with OFAC and following all its regulations, so we operated legally. Sarah was in Washington, DC, talking daily with the State Department and the Joint Chiefs. She also communicated regularly with members of Congress. She made sure we were doing everything properly and with approval.

For whatever motivation the State Department had, I think it figured out that the only way to shut down NGO evacuations was to allow the lily pad countries to max out on refugees they could handle. The vetting and processing to move refugees out of those countries came to a virtual halt. Our last flight of evacuees left three days before the deadline.

As I write this book, the State Department is still playing the same game to halt NGO efforts.

For that time, the rescues were over. Tim, Sean, Seaspray, and Dave returned to Abu Dhabi, and we reunited to share a meal, hold a debriefing, and address what was next for us.

I had badly wanted to fly back into Afghanistan one more time, even if just to help load evacuees onto one more plane. I had wanted to put my feet on Afghanistan dirt one more time.

But over ten days, when the dust settled, we had rescued more than twelve thousand people out of Afghanistan with, the best I can estimate, over fifty recovery operations. Only the Department of Defense evacuated more people.

And we saved Aziz.

Twelve

———— ★ ————

Unfinished Business

ON SATURDAY NIGHT, AUGUST 28, JOE, NICK, TIM, AND I accompanied our first group of evacuees to leave the UAE.

Another NGO had set us up with an Albanian official who said his country would accept two flights containing 350 evacuees each as a test, of sorts, that could lead to bringing more. EGYPTAIR provided the planes and volunteer flight crews.

I don't know if I've ever been on a happier flight! A new home represented a new beginning for all seven hundred on the flights. We interacted with so many of the Afghans on the trip. They knew who we were and what we had done, and they were beyond grateful. Many cried tears of gratitude. It was difficult accepting kindness from people who had lost so much. I was happy for them, but my heart still broke for them—especially for those traveling alone, like Ziagul, a young female whose family told her to leave because the Taliban had targeted her.

"Thank you for helping me," she said in broken English. "Now, can you help my family? I am a journalist, and my family didn't want me to stay because

I have been outspoken about women's rights. So, they told me to leave without them. Can you get my family out? They will kill them because of me. Please."

I told her we would do our best. What else could I say? We would.

Amid the smiles and laughs were reminders of the thousands still trapped in Afghanistan, like Ziagul's family.

Once again, elation and anguish mixed because for every story of one person rescued, countless more were waiting for someone—anyone—to help them.

The US deputy ambassador to Albania and Albania's interior ministry met us on arrival at the Tirana International Airport in Rinas. Both were excited to welcome the evacuees and seemed to have authentic and big hearts for the people. It felt good handing off our group to people who seemed to care for them. After our manifests were approved, the evacuees boarded buses for their next step in the process.

Nick and Tim had plans to drive to Greece to look into taking evacuees there. Joe and I were returning to Abu Dhabi but didn't have return tickets because we flew in unmanifested. The EGYPTAIR pilots said they were flying back the next day, and we asked if we could hitch a ride.

"Just call us and let us know," one said as he choked down one more of the many filterless cigarettes he had been chain-smoking since we landed. "We'll get you on the plane. No problem, my friend."

And then the pilots left for their hotel.

"What do we do now?" Joe asked.

A policeman had been assigned to us for, well, we didn't really know what for. He didn't seem to know either.

"I don't know what to do with you guys," he said.

Customs had closed for the night, so the policeman just opened the gate to the airport and the four of us walked out of the airport right into Albania. We caught a taxi and found a hotel where we grabbed about three hours of much-needed sleep. The next morning, we ate breakfast with an NGO representative overseeing the care and lodging of our Afghans. She took us to where the evacuees were being kept. It was a cool place in a pine forest, like a retreat or a church summer camp. Kids were playing outside, running around and laughing. Thinking back to my service time and remembering watching kids play in Afghanistan, I noted that the kids here didn't have to worry about stepping on a land mine. They were finally safe.

That's why we did this, I thought.

Tim and Nick left the camp and headed to Greece.

Joe and I took the two hours we had to spare to explore the war-torn city of Rinas. It was a simple city with kind people, Russian-theme architecture, and war-scarred infrastructure long overdue for repair. Bomb shelters had become tourist attractions. And, of course, Rinas offered some really good, authentic food, which made for a killer lunch.

As a taxi took Joe and me to the airport, I recorded a video to update the Save Our Allies followers on social media. I didn't reveal the country we were in because I didn't want to risk the State Department shutting down the possibility of us bringing more refugees into Albania. The deputy ambassador to Albania—a State Department employee—was awesome when he met us at the airport. Thirty seconds into recording, we pulled up behind a car driving ahead of us. I noticed a bumper sticker promoting the Biden-Harris ticket in the presidential election. I turned the camera to show the car. Halfway around the world, I said, we had found a Biden-Harris voter.

The Egyptian pilots had given us a time to meet them at the airport, and when we joined them, we asked how we could get through the gate without tickets and without being cleared through customs the night before.

The same pilot, smoking another filterless cigarette, said, "You guys follow us. We'll go where the pilots go through, and we'll take you with us like you are part of the crew."

Their plan didn't work.

Joe and I were stopped at the pilots' entrance and told we could not pass through without the proper ID. When we said we didn't have the ID, the head of security was called in. She was a high-energy woman with wild, curly hair and a giant skull-and-crossbones tattoo on her forearm. She listened to the security guard describe our situation, and the pilots validated our story. She was either on her second pot of coffee or her first line of cocaine, considering the pace she was moving at. She was on top of it.

"I am going to take care of you guys," she said in good English and a thick Albanian accent. "Don't worry, we will get you through."

"But we didn't go through customs when we got here," I said. "And we don't have a ticket."

"Don't worry," she said. "I am the head of security."

She showed us her badge to emphasize her point. This woman was serious about her job, acting like we were on a tight timeline even though with just the pilots and us on the flight, the plane wasn't on a schedule for departure.

"Follow me," she said and darted off.

She rushed us to the front of the line for bag screening, flashing her badge to the passengers waiting in line and the bag screeners to prove her authority to bump us to the front. Then we walked to customs, where she was not allowed to enter.

"Go through there," she told us.

"We haven't been through customs here," I told her again.

"Just go through," she said, unfazed.

The military wasn't the only place where I obeyed direct orders. She was clearly the boss.

Oh, man, this is going to be good, I told myself.

I handed over my passport, and the customs agent asked for my ticket. I pointed toward the tattooed, in-a-hurry head of security. She was my ticket.

"They don't need a ticket," she said loud enough for the man—and basically everyone else in customs—to hear.

He opened my passport, looked through the stamps, and placed my passport under the scanner. I didn't like the panicked look on his face.

"We didn't come through customs last night," I told him.

"How did you get in?" he asked.

"They just opened the gate and let us out," I said.

"Let me see yours," the agent said to Joe.

Same routine: he flipped through the stamped pages and scanned Joe's passport.

Same panicked look.

I leaned over and joked in a low voice, "We were never here."

Six-foot-tall Joe stood over my shoulder, shaking his head to the agent.

The agent took a step back, made a decision, and laughed.

"Just go," he said.

As Joe and I walked out of customs, I said, "Did I ever tell you about the time that we never went to Albania?"

Joe chuckled.

On the other side of customs, the security lady rejoined us, still moving briskly to make sure we didn't miss our unscheduled flight. We reached the gate, and the plane was not parked next to the jetway. We spotted it across the tarmac.

The woman looked at us.

"Do you have a yellow vest?"

"No, I don't have a yellow vest," I answered. "Why would I have a yellow vest?"

Fortunately, a rather large airport employee was nearby wearing a yellow vest.

"Give me your vest," she called out to him.

Although befuddled with the instructions, the man complied. We had one vest and two of us. The security head flagged down a bus driving toward us. She hopped onto the bus with us, pointed to our plane, and told the driver to take us there.

The bus driver pulled up next to the plane and, with us safely delivered and in plenty of time before our still-unscheduled departure, the woman finally seemed to relax. She smiled at us as we ascended the stairs to board, pleased to have completed her good deed for the day.

Our Albanian hero with a skull-and-crossbones tattoo!

We had arrived so early that Joe and I sat on the plane for two hours, eating lunch and trying to find ways to kill the rest of the time before returning to the UAE. We weren't used to having downtime and were eager to get back to Abu Dhabi.

Entering a New Phase

With no other places to take evacuees, I went on social media on Sunday, August 29, and informed our followers that Phase 1 of our mission—extraction—had ended. The beginning of Phase 2 shifted our focus to resettlement for every evacuee. We named this phase Operation New Hope.

We had evacuated 8,911 Afghans to the UAE and more than 3,000 to other countries, but the rescue work wasn't finished. The latest I had heard from the State Department was that about 350 US citizens were still trying to leave Afghanistan. Their numbers were never based on anything factual. I know I've been punched and kicked in the head a lot and even blown up a few times, but even I could detect the math to reach that number was nowhere near the truth. Our estimate was closer to 5,000.

The requests to help American citizens would keep flowing in. Even though our team had left Afghanistan, we had unfinished business there because there were innocent lives to be saved.

I had been communicating with young ladies named Maryam and Zahra. Maryam was twenty-two and Zahra was twenty-one. Their father was a pastor in an underground church. Because they were Christians, the family was known to the Taliban before the evacuations began. In the feeding frenzy after the US announced its withdrawal plans, the Taliban killed some of the pastor's family members. We were trying to help the family reach the airport, and the parents, one son, and one daughter made it into HKIA. They were placed on board a flight to the United States. But Maryam and Zahra could not get into the airport, and before the family lost contact with the girls, they directed the sisters to flee to Pakistan.

Maryam and Zahra made it to Pakistan on their own. When we reestablished contact, we arranged for them to stay in a safe house while we worked on a visa arrangement for them. They weren't safe in Pakistan either, because if identified they were just as likely to be raped and killed there if they weren't returned to Afghanistan and turned over to the Taliban.

I also had been working with Abdul Wasi Sharifi, an MMA promoter in Afghanistan and CEO of Truly Grand Fighting. MMA was a growing sport in Afghanistan thanks in large part to Abdul. A few of the fighters Abdul sponsored and promoted had made it to the United States to compete in the UFC and other major events. Abdul also had worked to help Olympic athletes and the Afghanistan national kickboxing team travel outside of their country to compete. The better training Afghan athletes received and the increased exposure they gained through international competitions brought more legitimacy to Afghanistan sports.

Taliban law, however, prohibited punching anyone in the face, and the Taliban demanded that athletes wear long trunks that extended below the knees. And, in a hefty amount of irony, the Taliban considered MMA too barbaric, which is irrationally contradictory for a group following a law that calls for the crucifixion or the amputation of a hand of someone who "wages war against Allah and his messenger" (Qur'an 5:33) or who commits theft (Qur'an 5:38).

Abdul was a solid business guy, and his work on behalf of Afghan athletes had made him a well-known public figure, especially in Kabul, where he lived.

Abdul had a wife and two precious, elementary–aged daughters. When the leash came off the Taliban, they issued death threats to Abdul and his family. The family went into hiding, and Abdul also moved his staff and MMA fighters into hiding. Because of my MMA background, Abdul contacted me. He forwarded one of the death threats to me and pleaded for help.

Abdul and I started exchanging communications, and his little girls melted my heart with a picture of them holding a handwritten sign that read, "Uncle Chad, please save us."

I not only told Abdul that we would help his family leave the country but I also asked him to send a list of MMA fighters, boxers, Olympic athletes, taekwondo competitors, and members of women's and girls' teams in other sports who were at risk under Taliban threats. When Abdul supplied the list, we arranged safe houses for as many as we could get in touch with. But the State Department closed the back valve before we could get any of them out of the country.

Save Our Allies also was among a coalition of at least eight organizations that received requests to help rescue the FIFA girls soccer team consisting of players aged fourteen to sixteen. Women and girls had enjoyed many freedoms after the Taliban had been removed from power, including education and participating in sports. Soccer, like many other sports, was growing in popularity. But with the Taliban taking over the country, the sport's future came to an abrupt halt.

We received video of an eleven-year-old who dreamed of becoming a teacher but instead was forced to marry a fifty-five-year-old man. The girl was resisting, digging her heels in the ground like any child would do when scared, as the man pulled her by her arms. Instead of trying to rescue her daughter, the girl's mother helped the man take her away.

The Taliban Cultural Commission had already dispatched an edict to all mullahs (Sunni Muslim clergy or mosque leaders who often serve roles comparable to a mayor) demanding they provide names of all young females in their areas age fourteen to forty-five, promising them to Taliban fighters as war booty. In essence, the Taliban was compiling a list of twenty million sex slaves. The soccer players would have been targeted as public examples and likely sent to reeducation camps and made brides for Taliban fighters.

Because of Afghanistan's economic collapse after the Taliban takeover, an estimated 22.8 million Afghans—which is over half the country's population—faced starvation in the winter after the United States left. Many families were selling young girls for as little as $500 so they could feed the rest of the family.[1]

It's sickening what the Taliban does with young girls and even young boys, to be completely accurate, and their sexual atrocities had eaten at me during my deployments. This was a battle we had to fight to free as many of these girls from evil oppression as we could.

With us out of Afghanistan and so many still in need of rescue, we needed to create new ways to evacuate people.

But first, I needed to go home for one of only a few things that could cause me to leave our operation: the honor of walking our only daughter, my beautiful Haili, down the aisle and presenting her to my very-soon-to-be-son-in-law, Andrew.

A man has no duty more important, no responsibility that's greater, than to those in his own home.

Thirteen

———— ★ ————

Power in Partnerships

I'M HERE TO ANNOUNCE THE COMPLETION OF OUR MISSION in Afghanistan."

With those words on Tuesday afternoon, August 31, General Frank McKenzie, the head of US Central Command, informed Americans that the final US military flight had left HKIA.

As I returned home for Haili and Andrew's wedding, safe houses became a crucial part of our efforts to continue evacuations. We worked closely with Rudy Atallah and Glenn Beck's team and other NGOs to move more people into safe houses, especially in the Mazar-e Sharif area of northern Afghanistan, which is a mountainous tribal area where the Taliban wasn't as active as other, more populated areas.

At one point, we NGOs were all spending $60,000 per day to safe house about four thousand people in that area. We flew a few chartered planes out of Mazar-e Sharif's international airport, but we're talking about hundreds of people leaving the country instead of tens of thousands. Every life mattered, but those numbers were well short of enough.

We worked with many organizations, like retired Army Special Forces Lieutenant Colonel Scott Mann's Pineapple Express group of veterans and aid workers, who were working from the United States to send people to safe houses in Pakistan through Pineapple Express's underground railroad network. We pursued every angle and option we could to move those vulnerable to places where they could be evacuated to safety, but we knew the Taliban would, at some point, stop the flights coming in and out of all airports, to include the small, rural fields used as runways in remote areas of Afghanistan. And safe houses weren't a long-term option because they were unsustainable financially and the Taliban was going door to door inspecting homes.

Seaspray, Sean, and I were planning an operation to fly out of Uzbekistan, jump into northern Afghanistan, and set up airstrips in remote areas where we could arrange evacuation flights for the people hidden in safe houses. Afghan commandos wanted to work with us. The plan was for Seaspray and me to parachute in during the middle of the night and meet up with commandos to hastily secure an area of land. Then we could fly in thirty-passenger planes as blackout flights under minimal lighting. We could get a couple of planes in and out before the Taliban could respond, and then we would move on to a different location.

We would need to make HALO jumps—high-altitude, low-opening parachute jumps the military uses to place troops on the ground quickly and undetected. My last military free-fall parachute jump came in 2004, and although I had more than 450 jumps logged, military free falls aren't like riding a bicycle. You can jump back on a bicycle after a long time off and be up to full speed in a few turns of the pedals. If only jumps were that easy. You must be sharp with all emergency procedures. Then, your body will be flying at terminal velocity, with all your equipment strapped to you. If you haven't jumped in a while, you likely will tense up during the fall. We call that potato chipping because your body flattens like a piece of plywood and wobbles through the sky instead of being relaxed, making it difficult to control the stability of your fall.

For a return to jumping after a long layoff, you typically refresh on emergency procedures and go into a wind tunnel to practice your body flying mechanics. The objective is getting good arch in your body and relaxing your arms and legs so you can grab the wind with your hands and feet to control yourself. Despite the danger involved, we used to laugh watching guys potato chip their first jumps after a long layoff. I wouldn't have an opportunity to practice before the operation though.

Seaspray was a certified tandem jumper, and we discussed a tandem jump. Tandem jumping is perfect for former president George H. W. Bush on his ninetieth birthday and for a girl's eighteenth birthday party. But with more than 450 free-fall parachute jumps to my credit, the idea of tandem jumping was a sting to my pride.

"I can't do that," I told Seaspray. "I'd rather burn in than be strapped to you on a tandem jump. I'll figure it out on the way down. I'll have a good twenty thousand feet to remind myself how to do this. That's plenty of time."

Following my short break for Haili's wedding, I flew to Washington, DC, for a summit that Sarah and The Independence Fund hosted for NGOs participating in Afghan evacuations and resettlement. Save Our Allies worked with a range of other organizations also operating in and out of Afghanistan. But events in Afghanistan had unfolded so quickly that there wasn't ample time for our groups to get together and strategize more ways to cooperate. I cannot emphasize enough how amazing these other groups' efforts were. Many people were accomplishing incredible feats driven by the same motivation as ours.

About a hundred people showed up for the summit. In addition to the NGOs, a number of congressional aides and representatives from the White House, the State Department, and the Department of Defense's Joint Chiefs of Staff attended.

Although we had lost access to the Kabul airport, each NGO present agreed to continue evacuations. We identified ways we could work together, because we knew that if we unified our efforts and finances, we would be much more effective. We also discussed options for moving people out of the lily pad countries, although the way people were stacking up in those countries was perhaps the biggest roadblock for all our groups, and the US government held all the cards.

The summit resulted in numerous partnerships that are still working together today. The only regret is that the chaos of the series of events in Afghanistan prevented us from getting together sooner.

Also, because of the summit, the State Department offered to hold a nightly conference call with representatives from each NGO for the State Department to provide us with updates. The calls could be viewed as an attempt by the State Department to gain more control over our work, and that might have been at least part of their intention. But starting the calls opened a daily line of communication for us with the State Department and created opportunities for us to scratch each other's backs a little, if you know what I mean. Even if we disagreed with almost all the State Department's actions, even the small percentage that we agreed on would be more helpful to our causes. As I write this book, the nightly calls continue, and they have greatly benefited our work. Additionally, Sarah has maintained ongoing dialogue with the Joint Chiefs and has briefed and spoken personally with General Mark Milley, who as chairman of the Joint Chiefs of Staff is the nation's highest-ranking military officer and principal military advisor to the president, secretary of defense, and National Security Council. General Milley isn't winning popularity awards over Afghanistan, and Sarah and I have caught flak over dialoging with him. But the truth is that the opportunity to work directly with the chairman of the Joint Chiefs has allowed us to accomplish much more than if we'd never engaged with General Milley or his office. General Milley even told Sarah in his office in the Pentagon, "I'm not abandoning this mission. I share the pain and frustration of veterans and I'm committed to protecting the investment we all made the past twenty years."

Our initial talks with high-level leaders in the government while in DC led to two important acknowledgments. CENTCOM, which oversees US military commands in the Middle East, acknowledged Save Our Allies' work during the rescues in Afghanistan. Any future criticisms that might be levied against us could be answered with CENTCOM's recognition of the organization. On-the-ground approvals and requests in Afghanistan could have been dismissed later as fog of war, but meetings with federal agencies gave Save Our Allies the credibility we had already earned.

At one point we were juggling requests for assistance from more than half a dozen federal agencies. The Federal Emergency Management Agency also asked Save Our Allies to provide humanitarian care, volunteers, and supplies for evacuees at eight humanitarian centers in the United States. That's when I learned that the federal government does not provide essential supplies such as food, clothing, diapers, and female hygiene products. Instead, they work with NGOs that can meet those needs. The government does, however, often provide grants to purchase those types of supplies. We took on the task of managing volunteers and services at the humanitarian centers. A key partnership with Team Rubicon developed from that responsibility.

Coming out of the summit and an internal strategy session, Save Our Allies developed four pillars to guide the work ahead of us:

- **Rescue:** We would identify US citizens, allies, and the vulnerable stuck in Afghanistan with no viable way out and whose lives, and families' lives, were endangered. We would rescue them through our assets and the assets of supporters and evacuate them to a safe location.
- **Settlement:** Evacuees were expected to remain in refugee camps, whether in the United States or overseas, from six to eighteen months for processing. We would place personnel at each refugee camp and help supply basic goods necessary for comfortable living. Our allies had left essentially everyone they knew and everything they owned in Afghanistan, and we wanted them to feel welcomed and comfortable during the lengthy transition to their permanent destinations.
- **Transition assistance:** When our allies gained their release from their refugee camp, they would face a tremendous learning process with limited resources to help them. We would assist their transitions into American life by helping them find housing, training, and employment.
- **Mental health:** Through our partnerships with Mighty Oaks Foundation and The Independence Fund, we would invest in the mental health of US troops and our allies who served in Afghanistan. Both groups had experienced trauma during their service, and we would ensure all could maintain emotional resiliency.

For all the good that came out of our time in DC, I returned home with a sobering statistic: high-ranking government officials shared with us that they'd been given a list of 175,000 people in vulnerable groups who remained in Afghanistan and needed to be evacuated.

All the NGOs still had much work to do—together.

While still in DC, I also met Dennis Price, who was serving as a Marine staff sergeant and team leader at 3rd Force Reconnaissance Company, a unit in which I had served. Dennis was at the summit through his volunteering with another NGO that had helped rescue smaller groups of high-value people.

Dennis was an impressive guy. He had received an award for Outstanding Force Recon Team Leader of the Year (an award not given lightly), had served multiple combat deployments, and had worked with other government agencies as a sniper in countries like Iraq.

The plans for Seaspray and me jumping into Afghanistan were progressing. Because of Dennis's reputation and experience, especially as a current jump master and HALO jumper, I pulled him in to draw from his insight.

In every good plan there are always naysayers: "haters," as my young-adult children might say. A few older operational guys also were part of our planning, and one was a hater who started armchair-quarterbacking the plan, calling it "cowboy stuff."

He chimed in, "Why would you do a HALO jump into Afghanistan when you can just have someone fly you in?" Clearly, he didn't understand the concept of clandestine insertion. While HALO insertions are great, for those jealous souls who don't get to do it, I guess they express their envy in downplaying their effectiveness. We weren't trying to come up with a plan that sounded cool. With the US military leaving and HKIA no longer a viable option, we needed temporary airstrips for flying planes discreetly in and out of Afghanistan, and a clandestine jump into those locations was the safest way to do it.

"If jumping in is a cowboy thing," I countered, "then why did the United States government spend millions of dollars training us to do it? HALO is the best insertion method for this."

Dennis remarked, "These guys complain about anything. You can be a water-walker, and they'll say it's only because you can't swim."

Dennis was my kind of guy.

Limited Options

I returned home, continuing to work the phones and email at all hours. We had rescue efforts ongoing and were ramping up our settlement work while also continuing to plan the air jump operation. But as we neared completing the plans, our option of using an airstrip in Uzbekistan dried up. Our only option now appeared to be creating land routes across borders for getting people out of Afghanistan.

As a large, landlocked nation, Afghanistan shares borders with six countries. Options for evacuees on foot were very limited. To the northeast, Afghanistan shares a stretch of border less than fifty miles long with China. The problem with China is, simply put, it's China. Moving clockwise from China, Pakistan is the next country and shares more border with Afghanistan—more than fifteen hundred miles—than any other country. Pakistan's prime minister had said a couple of months earlier that if the Taliban regained control of Afghanistan, Pakistan would shut down the border. We had successfully moved some Afghans into Pakistan, and others had made it on their own—like Maryam and Zahra—but Pakistan already was home to a lot of Afghans. We couldn't count on that country allowing more in. Plus, the route to Pakistan was extremely dangerous because Afghans' natural tendency to head to Pakistan had caused the Taliban to occupy all the border crossings.

Iran, to the west, had set up tents and shelters near the border for refugees but was already starting to send Afghans back home to the Taliban. Anyone who managed to make it into Iran would be returned home. Turkmenistan had placed troops along its five hundred miles of border with Afghanistan, cutting off passage to there. About 1,500 Afghans had already entered Uzbekistan, so it seemed like a good option. But with reports of Uzbekistan as a potential friendly option, the Taliban had beefed up its presence to secure that border. The chances of getting to the Uzbekistan border and crossing on foot were slim at best.

The sixth country was Tajikistan, which had announced it would accept one hundred thousand Afghan refugees plus ANA soldiers. The Tajik government also was talking about setting up refugee camps along the border and was building facilities for storing supplies in anticipation of a wave of border crossings. The border is close to nine hundred miles long, running from the tripoint with Uzbekistan to the west to the tripoint with China to the east, along the Amu Darya, Pyanj, and Pamir rivers and the easternmost section consisting of the Wakhan Corridor, with much of the border being the treacherous Pamir Mountains. When the Taliban took control of Afghanistan, Tajikistan had surged troops to the border. The Taliban strengthened its presence there, too, causing Russia to send more military to the Tajikistan side of the border. Everyone had their own interests in mind, and the border would have heavy military presence on both sides.

Dave Eubank—director of Free Burma Rangers, one of the most incredible human beings I know, and a longtime buddy of mine—was already in Tajikistan. When we were neck-deep in evacuations from HKIA, Dave called and offered help. But by the time he and his team would have arrived in the UAE, the US military would have reached the White House's August 31 deadline. I advised Dave to look for options to support border crossings and provide humanitarian aid, which is Dave's expertise because of his decades of work in war zones such as Burma, Iraq, and Syria. Dave had gone into Tajikistan two weeks prior and was accessing border crossings and setting up a humanitarian center near the border. I knew that area of northern Afghanistan well from my deployments. I was familiar with the mountains there and knew the Panj River that snakes back and forth between the two countries would provide great locations with routes offering cover and concealment for evacuees. Afghans were hiding in the Panjshir Valley, where the last Taliban resistance was located. A border crossing accessible from there made sense. We would have to account for the abundant Taliban checkpoints on routes to the border, but that area probably wouldn't be as dangerous as others—relatively speaking.

Tajikistan emerged as our most appealing option worthy of exploration. We decided a two- to three-man team should fly into Tajikistan, travel across the country to the border, and conduct a reconnaissance operation to identify border crossing points. Our intel reports could be shared with Afghan groups escaping and other NGOs and government agencies involved in helping with escapes.

I had performed the same type of operations in wartime during my deployments for my ▓▓▓▓ task force and likely was one of the few people experienced at this type of operation in this region. Andy's experience would have made a natural pairing for me, but he was busy coordinating the ongoing work in Abu Dhabi, and, in truth, he was a lot older and this would be a very physical operation. He could handle the role as operation controller from Abu Dhabi, but he could not make the trip. Tim and Seaspray certainly had the skill sets but already had commitments elsewhere.

I called my buddy Mike Glover, another former ▓▓▓▓▓▓▓▓ trained Special Forces sergeant major and sniper ▓▓▓▓▓▓▓▓▓▓▓ who owns and operates Fieldcraft Survival. Mike and I had been in touch a lot over the past few days, and I was able to get his longtime interpreter and family into a safe house and then on a flight to Abu Dhabi. Mike was not only a perfect choice operationally but he also had all the needed gear, such as GPS devices, Iridium satellite phones, and a list of all the outdoor adventure tools your heart could dream of. Mike is the premier outdoorsman from the Special Forces community, and he was all in. But after he reviewed travel itineraries, he unfortunately couldn't make the trip happen.

Our third man would now be my sole teammate, my recon brother and new friend, Dennis. We had hit it off the previous week in DC, and over the past few days I had learned more of his stellar reputation in the reconnaissance community. He was a trustworthy, legit operator, and because of his current and relevant real-world military experience, he would round out the years I had been out of the military. Also, Dennis was a husband and father of four beautiful children. He had nothing to prove and was not going to be in a hurry to get himself or me killed out of reckless bravado, and that was a big plus for me considering the type of operation.

When I asked Dennis if he was a go, he was ready to head to the airport.

Dennis just had to get permission from one person, his commanding officer at 3rd Force Recon Company, Lieutenant Colonel Tommy Waller, who just so happens to be a friend of mine. At the time, Dennis had just gone from active duty and into the Marine Corps Reserves' only Force Reconnaissance Company, and, as only God can arrange, I had been communicating with Colonel Waller throughout the previous six months about setting up an opportunity for me to speak to his Marines on resiliency. The collapse of Afghanistan had caused us both to shift our focus away from the resiliency briefing and toward helping those in need. Colonel Waller had been consistently helping us behind the scenes with resources, but perhaps most importantly with prayer. He introduced us to Intercessors for America, who began coordinating prayer calls with thousands of Americans across the country—calls dedicated specifically toward our teams and our allies we sought to save. I contacted Colonel Waller and asked if he could cut Dennis loose to help me in an unofficial capacity as a volunteer for humanitarian work rescuing Afghans. I didn't go into specific detail as to what the reconnaissance operation would entail, but I said our work would enable the future rescue of Afghans. I drafted and sent an official request to Colonel Waller, and Dennis received permission to accompany me to Tajikistan. We were all set.

Members of a US government intelligence agency that I won't name became interested in our operation and the intel we would collect. They offered to designate an agent to track us during our trip through a GPS monitor they would provide. The agency also said it would register us with the State Department to validate our travel into Tajikistan. But, they told us, we needed a cover story as our reason for traveling there since those in Tajikistan would certainly ask why we were there. That was a given.

I had already built a cover for why we would be in Tajikistan and how we could plausibly fit into the area. Since our meeting in DC, we had talked about how many current and former service members who served in Afghanistan were struggling mentally with Afghanistan's fall. Through my experience with PTSD and the knowledge gained through Mighty Oaks, I had helped Dennis process his emotions—and mine too. I had over 350,000 Instagram followers at the time; I couldn't hide who I am or claim to be someone or something I was not, due to my public profile. A simple Google search would bring up nearly anything about my military background anyone would want to know. We decided to lean into the truth of who I am. I had learned in my training and experience that a good cover is always as close to the truth as possible because it allows you to be more natural and not get caught up in a tale of lies that will crumble under a little digging or pressure.

My main job at Mighty Oaks is to serve struggling veterans. Dennis was the "struggling veteran," and I was mentoring him after the fall of Afghanistan. As avid outdoorsmen, we decided one of the most healing activities we could do would be hiking the border of Tajikistan and seeing the mountains of Afghanistan one last time as a goodbye, of sorts, to the blood, sweat, tears, progress of freedom, and loss of brothers. That part of Tajikistan drew extreme outdoors adventurers to hike in its mountains, so our story would seem natural there. I was confident it would work to get us where we needed to be and do what we needed to do.

The truth in that turned out to get us the exact access we needed.

Fourteen

————— ★ —————

The Exact Peace I Needed

JUST LIKE EVERYTHING ELSE OVER THE PREVIOUS SIX WEEKS, preparations for the Tajikistan trip ramped up in a hurry. With Mike out, we couldn't tap into his supply of gear at Fieldcraft and didn't have time to have it shipped to us. I headed to REI on a shopping spree to acquire gear for what we plotted out as ten days of hiking in mountains and swimming across rivers.

Tim's assistant drove to my Houston-area home to bring me Tim's Iridium satellite phone that included a Texas flag in the case. In exchange for using Tim's phone, Tim had a special request, and I vowed to take a picture of his Lone Star State flag on the Afghan border. (Spoiler alert: mission accomplished.)

On computers and during late nights, Dennis and I narrowed in on a ninety-mile stretch of the Tajikistan–Afghanistan border and searched for possible crossing spots using Google Earth, maps, and satellite imagery provided by some of our friends within the intelligence community.

We watched YouTube videos of the area and studied to prepare ourselves as best as possible in our short time frame. We had worked this way before during our separate times in the service, but Dennis and I were beginning to click like we had worked together on a hundred missions.

Watching me prepare for the trip started making Kathy uncomfortable.

"Why are you going to do this?" she asked. "You don't need to do this. Someone else can do it."

I tried to explain how my work in Afghanistan made me perfect for this operation.

"You haven't done this in a long time," she countered.

I couldn't disagree with her on that one. But I let her know that, just as I had to coordinate our operations in Kabul, I had to do this new operation in Tajikistan.

"You're going to go into Afghanistan, I know it," she said.

I couldn't lie to her. "Yes, I will have to," I said.

All the options for Afghans to leave the country were drying up, and somebody had to create more for them. Although Kathy was right that it had been a while, I had the unique skill sets and experience to get the job done in the quick time frame required. Every minute still equated to human life.

A series of conversations followed over the next few days. She was concerned about my age (I had just turned forty-six), and fourteen years had passed since my last recon operation.

I kept insisting that somebody had to help the Afghans. Even if Tim or Mike became available, they wouldn't fit the cover Dennis and I had established. I didn't know of anyone else capable enough and available to execute this operation. I didn't trust anyone else to either, and, truth be told, I didn't want anyone else to go but me. My heart felt pulled to go, and I had to.

Hunter expressed his concerns too.

I knew the operation would be dangerous. We'd have no cover. US government agency personnel would be monitoring us, and I'd be checking in with Andy every twelve hours, but nobody was coming to rescue us if anything went wrong. We would be sneaking across the border into Afghanistan. We'd need to identify Taliban checkpoints, so I knew we would come into close proximity to them. The Russian military would be in Tajikistan, and we'd probably encounter them. Who knew if there would be other foreign threats? We might see Chinese there. Although the government agency offered to provide pistols for defending ourselves, because of our cover, we declined and wouldn't carry any weapon other than a knife each befitting two hikers. I considered the chances of being searched during the trip 100 percent. We couldn't talk our way out of carrying pistols. A knife and the option of taking someone's weapon from them would be our only means of self-defense aside from good planning, wit, and the grace of God.

I say this with zero bravado, but I felt no fear. I wasn't nervous. I wasn't having bad dreams about the trip. I had peace. I was supposed to go, my mind was clear about what we were facing, and the peace I felt because of my faith and purpose was feeding into my confidence.

In one conversation, Kathy suggested I was going out of a desire to get back into doing the old macho things I had done before and that maybe I was missing all that stuff a little too much.

"I'm sorry this is so inconvenient for your life," I snapped. "But people are getting killed and raped over there."

Before the final words had left my mouth, I recognized the old Chad had reappeared. I was back to thinking people just didn't understand me. I had become too easily irritated, and I had become increasingly less compassionate toward Kathy and others. I had grown tired of people complaining about what, to me, were stupid things and inconveniences compared to what people in Afghanistan were going through. First World problems.

I apologized to Kathy. We asked our pastor and his wife if they could meet us for dinner and help us talk through our differences. They guided us through a great conversation that led both of us to gaining a better understanding of each other's perspectives. Kathy needed to realize that I wasn't going back to this type of work full-time, that this was a one-time trip vital to this season, and that I wouldn't be able to live with myself if I didn't go. I had to understand that Kathy couldn't relate to my feelings about Afghanistan because she hadn't been there, and she didn't know the people and circumstances the way I did. I had to accept that it was okay for Kathy not to relate, and that was a good thing for us. Why would I even want my wife to know that harsh reality or carry that burden? The truth is, I didn't.

Other than Kathy questioning whether I was trying to return to my previous macho ways, I also couldn't claim she was wrong about any of her concerns regarding the trip. I truly didn't feel I had anything to prove to myself or anyone else at this point in my life. I just had to do what I believed to be the right thing. She accepted that. We both still understood the danger involved.

Did we wind up in complete agreement about the trip? Of course not. We'd almost lost our marriage before, and in rebuilding our relationship, we learned that a strong marriage isn't built by always agreeing with each other but by how you handle your disagreements. We talk a lot about this in my marriage book, *Fight for Us*.

I had realized that Kathy was concerned because she loved me. She loved *this* Chad—the one who had put all his old ways behind him to mature as a man and become a good husband and father. I was focused on how much the Afghans needed me. She was focused on how much *she* needed me.

The two could coexist. Besides, what man doesn't want to feel needed by his wife, right?

But, just to show that our marriage is still a daily encounter with real life, we did have one more argument on the way to the airport.

"Kathy," I told her as she dropped me off, "you've got to hear me on this. What if this were our family? What if you were the one in Afghanistan? Or our sons were being forced to become terrorists? Or our daughter was the one who could be raped and enslaved? Wouldn't we hope for someone to come for us?"

Kathy listened to what I was saying. Later, she called and told me that although she still did not agree with me going to Tajikistan, she hoped that if it was our family involved in what was going on in Afghanistan, someone would help us.

That was exactly why I was going.

Losing Control?

From Houston to Frankfurt was a nine-hour flight—plenty of time to think. Maybe too much time to think.

I have a habit of counting down to big events and imagining the inevitable, whether it's good or bad. When I fought in MMA, I would visualize that I had twenty-four hours until I stepped into the cage to face my opponent. Then three hours. Then one hour. Then thirty minutes. My mental clock is always ticking down to my next big thing: the mental realization that something will come to pass.

From when the plane's wheels lifted off at the Houston airport, my mind was tracking the time until Dennis and I would arrive in Tajikistan's capital city, Dushanbe. Then we would take a seven-hour drive through the mountains to our first destination along the Tajikistan–Afghanistan border. I imagined my boots once again stepping on Afghan dirt, something I'd thought would never happen again. I was excited, not for the thrill of adventure but because of the deep burden tugging at my heart to do more for those stranded and hopeless.

Then I began thinking about how we would have very limited communications. I had never been in Tajikistan. I had never worked with Dennis. I was forty-six, and I hadn't undertaken this type of operation since 2007. The memories of my last deployment rushed at me. I was alone in the mountains, ████████ three days' travel from my unit on Bagram, but no one was coming to get me if necessary. I couldn't get to a hospital. Even a sprained ankle could have been life threatening. And then the VBIED had blown my home to rubble, and I had been stuffed into the car and interrogated ████, and then the crush of being brought home and diagnosed with severe PTSD, and I struggled with anxiety and depression, and my life spiraled out of control, and I almost lost my marriage, and then. . .

Now, I had chosen to place myself back into that environment.

My thoughts turned to my limbic system. I had studied the human brain structures that control our emotions, behaviors, long-term memory, and ability to use our senses. I needed to know more about what had happened to me. I needed to know how to explain to other veterans dealing with PTSD what was taking place physiologically inside their bodies so we could help them recover.

I had learned that I had no control over my limbic system if triggered. If one of my five senses triggered my limbic system, I'd be right back into fight-or-flight mode. My heart rate would elevate. My blood pressure would soar to dangerous heights. I could suffer a panic attack. Or a stroke. And then I would become a liability to Dennis.

I'd determined that I could physically handle our mission, but in my plane seat, I considered for the first time that I might not be able to do so physiologically. Was I endangering myself? My teammate?

Was Kathy right in telling me I shouldn't go?

I had to catch my breath and mentally take a step back from the onslaught of thoughts and questions. From the counsel I received at the height of my PTSD and panic attacks, I recognized that if I did not deliberately reject these thoughts and questions, I would be on the verge of losing control again. Doubt creates fear, and when fear takes root in the human mind it can take over and manifest those fears into reality. I had been there before.

But unlike back then, this time I had one more place to turn to for help: my faith. I know this well, have spoken to over 400,000 active-duty troops on this subject, and have even written a book on it called *The Truth About PTSD*. At this point in my life, I knew truth and knew just what to do.

God, I prayed silently, *You burdened my heart to be here. You've orchestrated all these incredible circumstances to make this operation possible, and now I'm on my way. This is supposed to happen because You have ordained this to happen. So, if You have placed this burden on my heart and ordained this operation to happen, then I need You to take away any fears, anxieties, and stress that I might face. Protect me from any physiological effects that my brain might have, and put me in a position to help Dennis build routes for these people to escape or be rescued.*

Before I concluded with "Amen," I was enveloped with complete peace again. It was the sort of peace where I could feel the protection of God's providential hand and the effects of the prayers of thousands of those supporting us, like those from Intercessors for America. I sent a picture of Dennis and me to Colonel Waller just before the plane took off with the message "Recon guys about to do Recon stuff." He immediately replied back that he was lifting us up in prayer with a request that we were each assigned an entire "fire team" of angels.

All these things contributed toward the peace I needed, but nothing more than my own conversation with God, which was a peace I had learned was like no other peace. It was a peace that the apostle Paul had described: "And the peace of God, which surpasses all understanding, will guard your hearts and your minds in Christ Jesus" (Philippians 4:7 ESV).

It was the exact peace I needed in that moment and for the trip.

Fifteen

---- ★ ----

Opposing Sides

DENNIS AND I MET IN FRANKFURT AND FLEW TO DUBAI together. In Dubai, we grabbed a few hours of sleep and began prepping for our arrival in Tajikistan.

We synced our GPS devices, checked our operations gear, and tested our Iridium satellite phones. We double-checked our maps and the routes we had planned. In addition to Google Earth, we now had the benefit of receiving live satellite imagery from the US government agency that wanted the intel we gathered. The government's real-time imagery would prove especially helpful in locating checkpoints.

Then we headed to the airport for our flight into Tajikistan. While we waited in the business center lounge, Dennis and I discussed how we had the same exact conversations with our wives on the way to the airport and joked about how they would get over it when we made it back home. Dennis and I had talked about our shared faith ahead of the trip and how he also felt called to Isaiah 6:8's words "send me" before he knew Save Our Allies had named our effort Task Force 6:8. I told him, "I think we should pray together for our trip before we take off."

"Man, that would be awesome," he replied.

We pulled our chairs next to each other and asked God to give us courage, open and close the doors that needed to be opened and closed, keep our minds sharp during the coming days of practically no sleep, and keep us safe. Then we prayed for the people who we didn't know but would be helped by the operation we were about to begin.

We landed in Dushanbe around 3 a.m. on Saturday, September 25. Dave Eubank had arranged for a driver to pick us up and take us to a safe house. We arrived an hour later—three hours ahead of a planned meeting with a local team that had offered to provide us with on-the-ground intel.

"Brad" from Free Burma Rangers had previously briefed us on the permits required for us to travel in the Gorno-Badakhshan Autonomous Oblast (GBAO), a large, densely populated, mountainous region of eastern Tajikistan bordered to the south and west by Afghanistan, to the east by China, and to the north by Kyrgyzstan. The region is largely autonomous from the Tajikistan government.

Brad was extremely helpful and accompanied us to obtain our GBAOs at the migrant police office in Dushanbe.

"It will be three hours," the clerk at the front desk told us.

"How much would it cost to get them sooner?" we asked.

"Come back in twenty minutes," the clerk told us.

For about the equivalent of five dollars in Tajik somonis, we saved more than two and a half hours and started our journey that day.

We then met with the local team to get the intel they were offering. They were also engaged in rescuing Afghans through different means. These were all some really good dudes doing great things for a solid organization, but they came across as a little territorial about us coming into Tajikistan. That's not uncommon for operators in such situations as this one and not something I would fault them for. If they are good, their operation should be priority to them, and it was. They informed us of a Russian military presence on the Tajikistan–Afghanistan border. A few of their teammates had been detained and questioned for twenty-four hours by the Russians. They also seemed too eager to persuade us that the Panj River along the border was uncrossable.

"If you get in the river, you'll be shot by the Russians because they have orders to shoot people in the river," one team member told us. "But it's impassable anyway because it is a Class V and the current is too strong."

A Navy SEAL corpsman from Free Burma Rangers who was with Dennis and me added that the river also was uncrossable because it was too cold from snow melt.

"The water is so cold," he warned, "that as soon as you get in the water, your body is going to cramp up and you won't be able to swim across."

The Russian military presence was a concern to us, but the river wasn't. As Recon Marines, Dennis and I had swum across a few rivers—including rivers flowing from snow melts. The fact that we were standing there among them served as proof we had survived. Fresh water freezes at the same temperature, regardless of whether you're in Afghanistan mountains or Colorado mountains, right? As long as water is moving, it isn't frozen. Sure, we would get cold, but we'd be fine.

As for the currents, even if the Panj was the equivalent of a Class V river (the second-highest rating on the difficulty scale) as described, the whole river wouldn't consist of rapids. We would look for points where the river current slowed or petered out and explore those spots for potential crossings.

It was clear these guys didn't want us working in their area of operation (AO). We thanked the team for the tea and information they offered, said we'd just have to explore for ourselves but would stay clear of their AO, and wished them the best with their operation. Despite any tension, I know they helped a lot of people, and we didn't want to get in their way.

With GBAOs in hand and fully briefed, we set out in an SUV with a team of four: Dennis, me, the driver, and a tour guide named "Nakita."

As tourist outdoors enthusiasts, we needed a tour guide so we wouldn't look suspicious. Andy had found Nakita, a dual US citizen ███████████ ████████████.

Andy over delivered. Nakita was a perfect fit for our team. She was about thirty, a free spirit, and spoke Pashto, Dari, Farsi, Tajik, and a little Russian. She had lived and guided in the United States, Tajikistan, Afghanistan, Pakistan, Iran, and other areas. She was intimately familiar with the eastern border where we were headed, and she was adept at using GPS for plotting locations. She was fearless, once hiking across Iran alone. Plus, as a female, she strengthened our cover instead of us being three military-age dudes out hiking on the Afghan border.

The autonomous region largely was neglected by the Tajikistan government, and limited road options made for a wicked trip through the mountains. Along the way, we came upon checkpoints both official and random. At the random checkpoints, police stopped us and requested a *baksheesh*—either a tip or a bribe, depending on the manner in which the request was presented—for passage. A few logged our identification paperwork, and others just wanted our money. Official checkpoints were typically manned by three members of the Tajik military, with two working the road and a senior rank of the guard inside the guard building. The stops were routine: the soldiers asked for our passports, our GBAOs, and paperwork for the vehicle. They asked our reason for being in the area and logged our information inside the guard building. At most, they gave a cursory look at us through the windows before waving us through.

Exploring the Border

After a long eight-hour drive from Dushanbe and through the mountains, we arrived at the border of Afghanistan in complete darkness, which prevented us from identifying potential water crossings until sunrise. We started driving the ninety-mile stretch of the border along Afghanistan's northernmost tip to collect data and monitor night security activity on the roadway.

The border was odd in that the Panj River zigzagged back and forth between the two countries. At times, the border crossed the road on which we were driving. We would be driving in Tajikistan and with no warning or marking suddenly be driving in Afghanistan for a short stretch. That area of those two countries was largely tribal, and the concept of a border wasn't important to most who lived there. But for us, it was an instant reality check of what we were doing and where we were. We were in "bad guy" territory.

We could technically be caught in Afghanistan while driving a Tajik road or "hiking" on this side of the river.

During the drive across the mountains, our phones had no cellular signal. But as soon as we reached the border, four bars appeared. The perfect service was not because someone decided to put a cell tower in the middle of nowhere; it was a signals intelligence effort to ping phones and electronically triangulate and locate people in the area. After a few calls came in from Russian numbers, it was pretty clear the Russian KGB was the culprit, and they were no one to play around with. A VPN doesn't help to disguise your location in such cases, so we shut off the cell service on our phones and hit our twelve-hour time windows using only our satellite phones or by using temporary locations and a short cellular data burst on encrypted apps like Signal. Because we had previously received intel that WhatsApp had been compromised by Pakistan ISI, which was feeding information to the Taliban, Signal was the most-trusted encryption.

We spotted a mix of militaries—Tajik, Russian, and, more to the east, Chinese. Plus, we saw Taliban fighters across the river. Fortunately, the militaries appeared to be treating the Panj River as the border, and the Taliban stayed on its side of the river. We recorded everything we observed about the militaries, including their numbers, uniforms, weapons, vehicles, and demeanor. We refer to these as SALUTE reports (size, activity, location, unit, time, equipment). In our jobs as Recon Marines, these reports helped paint a battlefield picture for upper-echelon commanders.

The focus of the military we observed seemed to be on guarding the river, not engaging with the public. Unless a driver, for some unknown reason, became belligerent and began honking his horn—which our driver did around 3 a.m. while Dennis, Nakita, and I were scouting a section of the river. He had grown tired of waiting on us, and his honking alerted nearby Chinese soldiers. I had to talk Dennis out of beating him up. After that fiasco, we called it a night and checked into a hostel that Nakita recommended.

The hostel, which actually was someone's home, had a balcony overhanging the river, and the hosts laid out bed mats for us on the balcony alongside the other guests. Dennis, Nakita, and I set up a rotating watch. The horn-honker couldn't be trusted, so we were going to let him get his sleep.

On a trip when we wound up sleeping just one hour each day and not in such luxurious accommodations as this hostel, this stop proved to be our only opportunity to grab three or four hours of sleep. Except the balcony floor vibrated whenever anyone moved. It seemed like every time the movements awakened me, I opened my eyes and saw Dennis looking back at me. So much for a decent sleep.

We woke up—for good—Sunday morning at dawn. I began my day as I would every day during this operation: reciting Psalm 23, which I memorized during a time of anxiety and depression and still say daily to myself as a reminder of its comforting truths.

> The LORD is my shepherd, I lack nothing.
> He makes me lie down in green pastures,
> he leads me beside quiet waters,
> he restores my soul.
> He guides me in paths of righteousness
> for his name's sake.
> Even though I walk
> through the darkest valley,
> I will fear no evil,
> for you are with me;
> your rod and your staff,
> they comfort me.
> You prepare a table before me
> in the presence of my enemies.
> You anoint my head with oil;
> my cup overflows.
> Surely goodness and love will follow me
> all the days of my life,
> and I will dwell in the house of the LORD
> forever. (NIV)

The hosts prepared breakfast, and other guests started joining us on the balcony to eat. They all were welcoming to us, and we decided to quickly depart before too many locals saw us and made us the talk of the town.

As we were leaving the hostel, we got our first look at what would be the daily morning dispatch of Chinese patrols along the river. We counted fourteen vehicles, a combination of armored vehicles with turrets and heavy machine guns for patrolling and high-back troop carriers to disperse troops along the border. We learned this was the time for a daily shift change relieving the nighttime troops, which is good information for planning operational movements around when troops are fresh or tired and complacent.

Sites to Behold

Before the trip, we had marked about two dozen potential fording sites, or crossing points, along that ninety-mile stretch. We drove up and down the border, instructing the driver to stop at places we had marked. Dennis and I then hiked along the river, evaluating for three requirements.

First, from the Afghanistan side of the river, we needed access to the river. This was a mountainous area, and Afghans couldn't simply have someone drive them down a road and drop them off at a crossing point. Also, a location could look promising on a map, but after traveling days toward the river an evacuee could discover it ended at a cliff one to two hundred feet over the river. Any potential crossing location needed a clear and safe path to the river. This is the same type of reports we would provide to military ground commanders as Recon Marines. If a regimental commander was moving an infantry battalion from Point A to Point B on the battlefield, they would need crucial human intelligence to gain a clear picture of routes, river crossings, bridges, and enemy and civilian activity, along with hundreds of other key points of information to help them in planning operations. The route and fording reports we were collecting were no different.

Second, the access point needed to be free of Chinese or Taliban checkpoints. It's easy to assume that this far north, the Taliban wouldn't care who left the country. But the Taliban has a convert-or-die mindset. According to the Sharia law the Taliban imposed, those trying to escape rather than to convert were "apostates." The penalty for apostasy is death, and the Taliban were enthusiastic about imposing that punishment on anyone they found trying to flee.

The Chinese had their own interest in not allowing Afghans to leave. The crossing had to be a path through all Chinese, Taliban, and other checkpoints along the river.

Third, we had numerous needs for the location itself. Because of areas of rapids and strong currents, the river had to be crossable. As a general rule, the wider a river is, the slower its current. But the river couldn't be too wide either. We had to find perfect in-betweens that offered slower currents and an easily passable width, knowing that the extremely cold water would be crossed by elderly, young kids, people who couldn't swim, and pregnant women. A lot of Afghan women are pregnant or have a newborn. The location had to provide cover and concealment as well as staging areas for families and small groups. Most of the time the people would cross holding on to a rope bridge, so both sides of the river needed to provide anchors—like large rocks—for the rope. And the entry and exit points could not be too steep.

Over the first two days, we narrowed our list to six potential fording sites and started camping at each one. To avoid being compromised in water, reconnaissance had to be conducted under the cover of darkness. Signs all along the border—seemingly in every language spoken in that area, and then some—made clear that swimming was forbidden. Even as tourist outdoors enthusiasts, we would not be able to offer a reasonable explanation for being in the water. There would be no first warnings issued to anyone caught in the river; you swam at risk of being shot. Other signs announced the presence of land mines along the river. Some of the signs probably were deterrents rather than the truth, but there was no need to discover for ourselves. At night, when temperatures were in the midforties, we camped on the riverbanks and measured the water's depth across the river's full width. Night also was the only time we could cross over to the other side of the river and collect data on the entry side.

When night became quiet in both Tajikistan and Afghanistan, Dennis and

I moved down to the riverbanks to gather as much critical intelligence as we could for future crossings. We would slip into the river to collect more information, then emerge into Afghanistan to do the same on the other side. Dennis and I had been plenty cold in our lives. The Basic Reconnaissance Course, the initial training to become a Reconnaissance Marine, holds its amphibious training in Southern California at Naval Amphibious Base Coronado. The frigid Pacific Ocean there crushes the dreams of many would-be Navy SEALs and Recon Marines, accounting for a large part of the 80 percent failure rate. Outside of training, Dennis and I had both operated around the world. Wet, cold, and miserable are staples of Marine Recon life. In 2006, I had been just south of where we were in the Himalayan Mountains ▮▮▮▮▮▮▮ at forty degrees below zero. Here I was again, on the Afghan side of the river, soaking wet at zero dark thirty, eating the whipping mountain wind for hours to plot grids and collect data and measurements while paying close attention not to get compromised by the Taliban. Good times!

As part of any fording report, we recorded detailed information and took photos. Latitude and longitude coordinates were plotted for entry and exit points of the crossings. We marked anchor points for rope bridges. We explored the cover and concealment. We examined staging areas. We identified vantage points—both good ones and deal-breakers. We recorded the various water depths of the river for each crossing, along with the direction of the current. We measured the current's velocity by throwing a floating object into the river and counting how many seconds it took to travel one yard. We even noted the soil composition of the riverbed entering and exiting the water.

One of the potential crossings was perfect in every attribute minus the Taliban and Chinese presence. But we deemed it worth conducting the reconnaissance anyway in case the Chinese moved. A Taliban checkpoint was visible across the river about one hundred yards east. Three guys with AK-47s were always on the roof of the structure. On this side of the river, about three hundred yards to the west, sat a Chinese BMP infantry fighting vehicle with a PKM machine gun on the roof and a giant spotlight and three Chinese soldiers. The best we could determine at that point was that there was one path across the river barely out of reach of the Chinese spotlight and just outside the

Taliban's vision, right in between them. Crossing there would be risky, but this information would be lifesaving for someone.

I remember being halfway across, swimming in a breaststroke to avoid splashing or making noise. I did long sweeping strokes with my arms and tried to breathe quietly as the ice-cold water contracted my lungs. I kicked hard under the water against the current and felt a sharp pain in my injured groin. This was not a good time for my groin to fail me. I switched to sidestroke, another efficient and stealthy technique that seemed to take the sting out of my groin across the river and back.

Another night we stopped at one of the fording sites to cross the river. Dennis wanted to take pictures from where the car stopped. In our training, we learned to watch for shapes, shines, or silhouettes that seemed out of the ordinary. As Dennis was getting out of the car with his camera, the moonlight revealed twenty yards in the distance a large square that didn't fit the surrounding vegetation. I looked closer and noticed the square was fresh vegetation placed to cover a mechanized armored vehicle. I immediately spotted the Chinese soldier next to it—not regular military, but probably special operations—wearing a ghillie suit with fresh natural foliage to blend into the vegetation. The soldier was holding what appeared to be a sniper rifle and staring directly at Dennis. I grabbed Dennis by the back of his shirt and pulled him back into the SUV while ordering the driver, "Go! Go! Go!"

The driver sped away, not knowing why we needed to get out of there but understanding he needed to hit the gas pedal first and ask questions second.

We moved on to a new location, where later Dennis and I were sitting by ourselves along a riverbank. The river was fairly narrow, about seventy yards wide. A Taliban checkpoint was directly across the river, and three Taliban were patrolling that side of the river with flashlights. Dennis and I concealed ourselves by sitting against a big rock as we waited for the Taliban activity to subside so we could get to work on gathering more data.

I've been in the Colorado mountains, and the beauty of the night skies there is stunning. But they don't compare to the skies above the mountains of Tajikistan and Afghanistan. I felt like we could see every star in the galaxy.

The river was alive in that spot, so we were able to talk in somewhat hushed tones. We started out talking about plans related to the operation, but before long, the conversation steered more personal. Our fording and route recon were fundamental reconnaissance missions. They were old-school missions, the bread-and-butter work of our trade, and it was cool that Dennis and I, from different generations of the Marine Recon community but trained the same, had clicked like longtime teammates after only a few hours together. Add in that Andy, back in Abu Dhabi monitoring us every twelve hours, was a Recon Marine from a generation before me, and I wondered if three generations of Recon Marines had ever conducted such an operation together.

I liked Dennis after meeting him two weeks earlier. He was pretty intense but big-hearted and highly intelligent. He loved talking about his wife and four kids. I could tell he was a great husband and father. Dennis also was a funny guy with a dash of dark humor. Serving in the military tends to bring that out in you. Maybe it's a way to deal with the stress or just the personality type that is drawn to the trade. But Dennis took every second of operations seriously and was a high-level professional down to every detail. It made me proud to see the next generation of where I had come from function at such a high level under these circumstances.

I shared with Dennis my memories of the first time my feet touched Afghanistan soil at Bagram. It was nighttime then, too, and I walked out to the edge of the HESCO barriers and concertina wire and looked out into the darkness.

This is for real, I remembered thinking. *I'm really in combat now. The Taliban is out there. They're going to try to kill me, and I'm going to try to kill them.* It was a moment I'll never forget when the gravity of really being in a war zone hit me for the first time. Dennis said he knew exactly how I had been feeling, and we were both experiencing it again. Seventeen years later, an old Recondo sitting next to a younger one, the same enemy in sight. Death was seventy yards from us. The Taliban didn't know, but we were there together with them, under the same sky, doing our jobs under the light of the same stars while under the watchful eye of the same Creator.

We had so much in common as warriors doing our duty, but we were divided by so much more than this running river.

Sixteen

———— ★ ————

Saved by a Selfie and a Cigarette

THE BORDER PRESENTED A STRONGER MILITARY PRESENCE than expected based on our predictions and initial intel we'd received.

First, there were the Tajik and Russian militaries. Tajikistan has long ties to Russia, dating to the Russian Empire's conquest of Central Asia in the nineteenth century, and it was part of the more modern Soviet Union until gaining its independence in 1991. The Russian influence remains.

Tajikistan's economy is fragile, and many of the people financially depend on family members who migrate to Russia for work and send money back home. Although Tajik is the official language, Russian is widely spoken, including in government and business.

The Tajik military uses old Russian and Soviet-era equipment and newer Russian hand-me-downs, and the Russians' largest international military base is near Dushanbe.

Tajikistan is landlocked and, slightly smaller than Wisconsin, is the smallest nation in Central Asia in terms of area. But Tajikistan is strategically located for Russian interests because of its lengthy border with Afghanistan. Any destabilization of Central Asia by the Taliban poses a threat to Russian interests and could prove to be a drain on its military resources. Also, drug trafficking from Afghanistan through Tajikistan and into Russia has long been a problem that will only worsen with the Taliban controlling Afghanistan.

Since the US withdrawal, Russian president Vladimir Putin has called the Tajikistan–Afghanistan border a concern for his country and has vowed military support for the Tajiks.

That explains the Russian military presence we observed in such a strong show of force.

We didn't believe the Tajik military to be much of a threat. We commonly spotted them in foot patrols of three to six soldiers dispersed about fifty yards apart along the road running next to the Panj River. They were dressed in Tajik green-and-yellow digital camouflage and tended to be what I would call relaxed to complacent, carrying their Soviet-style arms behind their backs or on their shoulders, nearly dragging them on occasion. A few times we observed a marksman or sniper in all-black fatigues accompanying patrols.

The Tajik military seemed interested only in guarding the river. The area was sparsely populated, so the only groups of people they would encounter in that area were either locals or tourists on extreme outdoor adventures (like us, supposedly). From time to time, we offered touristy waves to the Tajik military that were, more often than not, returned with waves and, every once in a while, smiles. As long as we had all the required paperwork and acted like we belonged in the area—no swimming in the river!—we were good with the Tajiks.

The Russian military, not surprisingly, was a little more serious looking and less friendly toward us tourists. Their focus also was on the river, and we surmised that if we managed to get sideways with the Russians, the worst they would probably do was arrest us and kick us out of the country (not that we wanted to test our belief). But the higher-than-reported numbers of Russians posed problems for potential rescue attempts across the river in certain areas.

On one occasion, we witnessed a convoy of twelve BTRs (Russian tanks) and twenty-seven high-back trucks carrying troops toward the border. Up in the mountains, we heard pop shots coming from both sides of the border that we figured to be Russian snipers hunting the Taliban.

The Tajikistan and Russian military would not want us in the area and would have dealt with us accordingly. But the Chinese posed a much bigger threat, and we saw more of the Chinese than the other militaries.

The Tajiks would have had to allow the Chinese to be on their side of the border, and I'm not sure why they did. The Chinese were working with the Taliban to keep Afghans from leaving.

We observed different types of Chinese troops. There were what we called the rock-kickers—the ones who stared at the ground and kicked rocks to pass the time when patrolling along the road. They had their rifles slung over their backs and were grouped in patrols fifty yards apart. Then there were the ones in ghillie suits and carrying sniper rifles both patrolling and concealed in bushes alongside the river. We also saw numerous mechanized vehicles hidden by natural vegetation brush with mounted heavy machine guns and large spotlights for catching people in the river.

Based on numbers, the Chinese weren't playing around. If they caught us, they would know what we were up to and would have enjoyed turning us over to the Taliban, or maybe worse.

Then, across the river, the Taliban were active with patrols, checkpoints, and at posts flying Taliban flags. Every time we entered the river or crossed to the other side, our lives were in jeopardy. There were no military orders for us to be there, only a compulsion in our hearts to help those on the other side—scared, helpless, and blind. No government in the world was coming to help them, and I couldn't help but think back to the question I had posed to Kathy at the airport: What if my family and I were in their situation? Would someone come for me and my wife and children? I sure hoped so.

Beauty in Simplicity

Being in Tajikistan rekindled my love for the simplicity of the culture I had experienced in Afghanistan.

One day, Dennis and I were out alone driving into a remote location. We came upon a small village and stopped when we saw a big awning, about fifteen feet by fifteen feet, with mattresses underneath. It was a spot where the locals gathered with their neighbors during the day to drink tea and socialize. Or nap. Dennis and I joined in to relax, kick back briefly, and recharge and focus for what was ahead.

I grew up in a part of southern Louisiana—Bayou Country—where the lifestyle was simple. People familiar with where I grew up would call me a coonass, slang for people who live off the natural resources of fish and game from the swamps and bayous. That awning in Tajikistan and similar villages in Afghanistan always took me back home, to where the people were self-sufficient. They owned property with water wells, and they fished, hunted, raised animals, and grew vegetables. Some worked only five or six hours a day—although it was hard work—and spent the rest of the day with family and neighbors. They didn't have a "real job," some would say, and wouldn't have wanted one anyway because it would have interfered with the way life was supposed to be enjoyed.

Back before we killed Osama bin Laden, I used to chuckle at the $25 million reward the US government offered to anyone who provided information leading to bin Laden's capture. When we got bin Laden close to ten years after 9/11, we found him through electronic intelligence, not human intelligence. For all those years, there seemed to be this unspoken curiosity about why the $25 million wasn't enticing anyone to turn on bin Laden. From my time embedded with the Afghan people, I believed I knew the answer. The Afghans had to wonder what they would do with all that money. Build fires with the cash? They didn't have much money, and their lifestyles didn't require much money. They didn't want the money. They could live off the land, and when they needed help, the neighbors would take care of them. And then they would do the same for their neighbors when necessary. Their lives were beautiful in their simplicity.

It's not that I wanted that lifestyle for me, but I always admired those who lived that way, whether they were from my hometown in Louisiana, or in Afghanistan and Tajikistan living the way their families had lived for thousands of years. It's hard not to envy their lifestyle just a little.

Dennis and I wrapped up our tea and paused to air out our feet in the shade of the awning. Then we resumed our drive because people were at war against one another and lives were in the balance. I contemplated how money meant power, and the pursuit of power caused violence against fellow man. Perhaps if our world had more awnings and mattresses, we would have a lot less war. But even in the simplicity, war didn't escape these people.

Duct Tape, Zip Ties—and a Marker

The multiple military units present practically within eyesight on most of our ninety-mile route made finding a safe location for passage difficult. We had narrowed our list of two dozen potential locations to six worth exploring, and the amount of data we had recorded created too much of a risk if we were detained near the border.

We drove back to Dushanbe to begin writing up our fording reports and regroup for a return trip. While there, Dennis received a request from a Marine concerning an Afghan family of four that was on the move to attempt crossing the Tajikistan border. The wife was seven months pregnant, and their two children were fifteen and three. The father was an Afghan commando who the Marines had served with, and the Marine was helping his Afghan ally escape. Americans had highly trained the commandos for special operations, and they were targeted by the Taliban not only to be killed but to gather critical intelligence on tactics and tradecraft. Reportedly, 5,600 commandos and their families were hiding in safe houses in the mountains waiting for the US evacuation they were promised. This commando had been flushed out and was on the move.

Dennis felt compelled to help.

"Let's try to get them across," Dennis suggested.

Executing rescues was not our reason for being here, but how could we not help this family after just building a route out for this very reason?

"Let's do it," I said.

We needed two SUVs and two vetted drivers. Matt Nelson, a retired Marine Corps Intelligence colonel, had provided us with maps, live satellite imagery, and logistical help, and he said he could secure vetted drivers and vehicles for us.

157

Because the mother was pregnant, Nakita recommended we take along a nurse named "Sasha." She said Sasha spoke Tajik and Russian and had delivered babies. Nakita contacted Sasha, who happened to be on vacation in the region, and asked if she would like to see the Panj River and possibly help some Afghan refugees after they crossed the border. Sasha enthusiastically agreed to join us.

Dennis and I compiled a list of the gear needed for a crossing and went to a small hiking store. I asked the one employee if he had repelling rope.

"No, we're out," he told me.

I looked along the floor and spotted a spool of bright orange rope tucked away almost out of sight.

"You have one right there," I said, pointing to the spool.

"Oh, I didn't know we had that," he replied.

"Do you have any other rope?" I asked.

As he was saying, "No, I didn't know we had that one," I saw a red rope hanging in a display along the far wall.

"God," I said to myself, "You have answered our prayers." But in God's humor, I think He might have chuckled with providing me bright orange and red rope—not the most discreet colors for a clandestine nighttime river crossing.

I asked the employee if he sold dark spray paint.

"No, we don't," he said.

At this point, I had to look for myself. But I didn't see any around the store, so we had to pick up spray paint elsewhere.

We also purchased medical equipment and carabiner clips and D-rings for securing the rope to the family members. I was concerned about the cold river causing the pregnant woman to panic or go into labor because if she screamed, she could get us all killed. I grabbed an inner tube that we could put over her head and down to the top of her belly to float and tow her.

Just in case Chinese or other soldiers came upon us, I told Dennis we also needed to buy duct tape and zip ties.

"And a magic marker," he added.

"Why a magic marker?" I asked.

"After we duct-tape and zip-tie them, we can draw penises on their heads," he said. "When their buddies find them, they'll be made fun of for the rest of their lives."

We purchased one marker.

Any Taliban that compromised us would not receive the same courtesy of detainment as the Chinese.

When we returned to the safe house, Brad from Free Burma Rangers told us they had a good rope and carabiners we could use, plus a small river raft in lieu of a tire tube. We were able to trade what we had for good gear and didn't have to spray paint the ropes. But we did pack our abduction kit—including the marker.

Dennis and I recruited a guy named "Jake" as an interpreter because he spoke Pashto, Afghanistan's other official language along with Dari. Jake had served in Afghanistan as a Marine and fell in love with the culture while learning the language. Because Jake worked for Free Burma Rangers, he was limited in how he could participate in the rescue itself. But in addition to interpreting, Jake would be useful in keeping timelines and staying with the drivers to ensure they didn't leave if we wound up engaged in intense action.

But we hit a snag with the drivers. With things happening so quickly, Matt was unaware of the need for GBAOs where we were headed. GBAOs were mission critical because without one, a driver would basically be limited to driving around Dushanbe.

Dennis turned to Nakita, who had a list of backup drivers just in case. We called the manager of a tour company Nakita trusted and had worked with for many years. We vaguely described the nature of our trip. We emphasized that we needed trustworthy drivers who wouldn't bail on us and that we were willing to pay what it would cost. The manager assured us that would be no problem, and within a few hours, two drivers in two SUVs arrived and helped us load our gear. We headed east with Jake and a driver in the first vehicle and Dennis, Nakita, Sasha, and me with the second driver.

Thanks, Gomer!

On the way to the border, we stopped at a Tajik–Russian military checkpoint. We'd had a little fun at this same checkpoint on our return to Dushanbe. We had rolled down our windows, and while they checked our paperwork, they started asking the usual questions about who we were and our reason for traveling into the area.

I interrupted their questioning with my own questions.

"Are you guys in the military? Policemen? Or what are you?"

They seemed taken aback, and one reluctantly answered, "Military."

"That is so cool!" I said. "I love the military. Do you like being in the military?"

The one-word first answer must have been the most they were allowed to say because they showed no interest in engaging in conversation.

That just upped the ante as far as I was concerned.

"It must be a cool job to be here! It's so beautiful out here!"

No response.

I noticed one of the guys wearing bright, camouflaged boots. I pointed to his feet.

"That guy—I really love those boots! It would be really cool to take a picture with you guys. Can we get out and take a picture with all of you?"

The checkpoint guards nodded, and we hopped out of the car for a picture.

The one in the flashy camouflage boots must have been flattered by our compliments because he snapped to attention for the photo. I didn't notice at that time, but when I was looking at the photo and laughing at the memory, that soldier resembled one of America's most-beloved Marines, Gomer Pyle.

I thought about asking to hold his rifle for a photo but didn't want to push my luck.

Before we left, Dennis offered the guys cigarettes. Dennis didn't smoke, but he had brought along cigarettes and medicine because he knew they were great tools for making friends and earning favors.

My new friend took a cigarette.

On our way back to the border through that same checkpoint, for the first time on the trip, Dennis and I were asked to get out of our SUV. In the dark of night, three armed soldiers escorted us into the guard building, closed the door, and stood between us and the door.

An officer with three stars on his shoulder was seated at the desk in front of us. He looked up from his paperwork. Even if he hadn't been wearing stars, his stern expression and mannerisms would have sufficiently announced his senior status.

He flipped through our passports and GBAOs.

"You can't come through here," he declared.

"What do you mean we can't come through here?" I asked.

"You don't have the right paperwork," he responded, handing our papers back to me.

"We have the right paperwork," I said.

"No, you don't," he shot back. "There is another form you need from the airport. The information is right, but it needs to be signed. You have to go back to the airport and get that done."

I intentionally turned as argumentative as any upset outdoors-loving tourist would be in this situation.

"The airport is seven hours away. We have everything right. We have the right to go through here. Why won't you let us through?"

At that point, Mr. Three Stars wanted to end the discussion.

"Sorry," he said, unconvincingly. "You have to go back to the airport."

"Look," I said, reaching for my trump card. "I don't want to get anybody in trouble here if we're not supposed to go through here. But this is our third time through, and you guys let us through twice before. Our names are in that logbook on your desk. I don't want to get anybody in trouble, but when I go back to the airport and tell them we have been through here twice and now you're saying we can't go through—"

I glanced over at Dennis, who looked ready to start stabbing people.

"You didn't come through here, and your name is not in this book," the officer said.

"Open up that book," I said. "Our name is in there."

"No, you didn't come through here," he replied. "You must be confused. It must have been a different checkpoint. We would have never allowed you through here."

In all our work associated with missions to rescue people from Afghanistan, I would not even want to attempt to estimate the number of little moments that popped out of nowhere and opened a path where one did not seem possible. Another walked through that door right then. It wasn't an angel coming to our rescue, but it was the next best thing we could hope for in that moment—our friend, Gomer Pyle.

He obviously knew what was going on and decided to join in on the fun.

"You let us through here," I stated, pointing to Gomer.

"No, it wasn't me," he said.

"Oh, yes, you did," I told him. "We took a picture together."

I quickly thumbed to our group picture on our phone, extended it forward, and moved my hand around so everyone in the room could see the flashy-booted soldier and his buddies posing with Dennis and me.

"This is you in the picture," I said.

The officer looked at Gomer with a "You idiot" expression.

"This is him," I continued. "We took a picture with him at this checkpoint right here, and you let us through."

"Yeah," Dennis added, "and I gave you a cigarette."

The other guards broke out in laughter. The officer shook his head and motioned for our paperwork. I handed everything back to him, and he quickly signed where needed and handed the papers back to me.

"Go," he said, giving us a shooing motion with his head still down.

And we did. Quickly. Before anything else could go wrong.

Seventeen

———— ★ ————

Going Swimming!

I GUESS YOU SHOULDN'T EXPECT MUCH PRIVACY AT A dollar-a-night motel.

We arrived near the border early the next morning and checked into a motel that had two large rooms: one for men and one for women. As in every male guest in one room and every female guest in the other.

Our guys joined a handful of men already sleeping on the floor.

About an hour after falling asleep, we woke up to a sound I couldn't quite make out. It sounded like someone chopping, but it definitely wasn't the sound wood makes as it's being split. I walked outside to investigate and found a man standing next to a propane bottle wildly swinging an axe into what looked like a spinal cord and ribs off some kind of beast. The way he swung made him look like some crazy guy right out of a low-budget horror movie. *The Hills Have Eyes—Afghan Edition.*

I walked off to a spot in a rocky draw coming off the mountainside where I could be alone and think ahead to our attempt that night to rescue the Afghan family. We hadn't come to Tajikistan to rescue anyone. We had come to find ways to rescue people or provide lifesaving data for them to escape themselves. Although confident in our reconnaissance, we hadn't made a dry run without placing anyone other than ourselves at risk of being captured and killed. We believed our plan would work but had yet to prove it would. There's a big difference between the two.

But this family needed us—now. We might be their only hope of being rescued. We had to try.

The Lord is my shepherd, I shall not be in want, I began praying.

After concluding my daily recitation of Psalm 23, I felt that deep peace and began my walk back to the motel.

The crazy axe-swinger was now cooking the fruits of his labor.

It turned out he had been chopping a goat, and the goat meat was mixed in a broth with potatoes and fresh onions over the propane tank's flame. The food smelled great. And when the man had finished his work, he distributed breakfast to the guests. The mountain goat soup tasted amazingly delicious—the best goat I've ever eaten, for as little as that's worth.

At this point, we had identified one primary location as good for crossings. However, the route the family was taking through the mountains would force them into a Taliban checkpoint. The family did not have a plausible reason for passing through the checkpoint, so we decided sending them to that crossing point was too risky.

We had one spot from our original list that we hadn't checked yet that aligned perfectly with the family's route, which would pass through a friendly homestead that could serve as a hiding place.

We set out early in the morning for that location. This was one of those places where the zigzagging border brought the road into Afghanistan. We pulled off the side of the road, and our immediate reaction was that this could be the best spot of all. With a few hundred yards of tree line, vegetation was plentiful for concealment. The river was narrow yet slow—about fifty yards wide. Everywhere else we had checked with a similar width had much faster currents. The water was so calm that we might not even need a rope bridge. Instead, we could probably swim across with a rope or tie the rope onto our small raft and pull the raft with evacuees inside across the river. But if we did need to establish a rope bridge, both sides had sufficient rocks for anchors.

Both sides also offered great entrance and exit points. Most important, the other side had a waist-high rock wall that would provide excellent cover.

We needed to conduct a more detailed recce (jargon for reconnaissance), though, before determining this was the place to meet the family.

We had established a safe location in a hostel near where Dennis had met two friendly locals, Islamadad and Mochmaboch, working in a small restaurant. He arranged for the two to take him and Nakita on a hike up the mountain to gain a better vantage point where he could take pictures. He specifically needed to confirm or deny Taliban checkpoints, determine the Russian and Chinese presence, and monitor Tajik troop movement and posts. Meanwhile, I drove the routes along the river in both directions of the potential crossing to identify military presence and activity.

When Dennis, Nakita, and the two locals reached the military crest—the area below the topographical crest where maximum observation is possible— Dennis stood in an open area to take photos. A few seconds later, he heard a snap and saw rocks kick up about twenty to twenty-five yards from him.

"There are snipers in the mountains," the locals told Dennis.

A second snap rang out, and more rocks scattered.

Dennis is not only a Recon Marine but a scout sniper instructor with the highest level of sniper training in the world. He knew the shots were from a 7.62 caliber rifle. The shots probably came from a Chinese or Russian sniper firing warning shots at what they suspected were tourists. If the sniper had wanted to hit Dennis, he probably would have. He definitely succeeded in running Dennis off from his observation point. Dennis and company immediately headed down the mountain.

We met up again at the hostel and discussed our findings. The location still looked great for a crossing, but we hadn't been in the water to measure its depth, gradient, and current or crossed over to the other side to verify our observations. But we did not have time to wait until nighttime to get into the river and collect the missing information before the family arrived.

"We need to get into the river in the daytime," I told Dennis.

"If we get into that river, we're going to get shot," he responded.

Dennis brought up Islamadad and Mochmaboch. Perhaps they could be of help, he said. Dennis returned to the restaurant and engaged in a conversation with Mochmaboch.

"Can you swim?" Dennis asked him.

"I'm a good swimmer," Mochmaboch answered. "I swim all the time."

"Where do you swim?" Dennis asked.

"Anywhere."

Dennis pointed to the river.

"Yes," Mochmaboch said. "All the time."

"How do you not get shot by the Taliban or the Tajiks or Russians?"

"It's okay," Mochmaboch assured. "I do it all the time."

Then Mochmaboch asked if Dennis could swim.

"I'm an excellent swimmer," Dennis answered, hoping Mochmaboch would take the bait.

He did.

"I will take you swimming there now," Mochmaboch offered.

Dennis played along, saying he didn't want to get shot.

Mochmaboch repeated that he knew where to swim without getting shot because he knew the Taliban posts' locations and the patterns of the Tajik and Russian military patrols.

Trap sprung, Dennis agreed to go swimming with Mochmaboch. However, Mochmaboch was mentally ill, and we would need to also sway a landowner—hopefully a sane one.

Over lunch, we continued to plan our rescue operation, and then Dennis and I packed swimming trunks into our day bags.

A Cow, Fruit Trees, and One Cold Cannonball

Dennis, Nakita, Sasha, and I met up with Mochmaboch and Islamadad and walked across the street to the farm Islamadad and his brother owned. The farm, which was in Afghanistan even though it was on the near side of the river, consisted of about three acres with two compounds—a main residence for the brother's family and a small guesthouse. Islamadad's brother introduced us to his wife and three daughters, and we sat down to drink tea. They were typical Afghans—friendly, hospitable, and honored to have guests in their homes.

"Your property is so beautiful. I really love this place—I can't believe you get to live here," I said, making sure to lay the compliments on thick. "We would love to walk around and see your property if that's okay."

Islamadad and his brother promptly took us on a tour. We observed one cow and no dogs. If we brought the family across this property, we wouldn't have to worry about a barking dog at night.

A variety of fruit trees dotted the property.

"Can we buy some fruit from you?" I asked.

"Eat what you want," the brother said.

We took him up on the offer. The pomegranates and plums tasted delicious.

"Man, I just can't get over how beautiful your farm is," I said. "This is a great place to live. Can you take us to see the river? It must be so beautiful down there."

"Sure," the brother said.

We walked down to the river, and Dennis and I were so going swimming.

"I can't believe you live right on the river," I said to the brother. "Do you and your kids get to swim here?"

"All the time," he said.

"Wow!" I said. "It must be so amazing to get to swim here."

"Do you want to go swimming?" he asked.

Why, I thought you would never ask!

"I don't know," Dennis said, repeating his tactics from his conversation with Mochmaboch. "I don't want to get shot. You know there are Russian and Chinese military out there."

"Oh, no," the brother said, "you won't get shot. Not if you are with me."

"What about the Taliban?" Dennis asked. "Will the Taliban shoot us?"

"What about getting arrested?" I said. "I don't want us to get arrested. You know we aren't supposed to go into the river."

We were playing up our lack of eagerness to a tee, but inside we were already getting cold and wet.

"If you go in the river with me," the brother assured, "you are my guest. I would just say you are my guest, and no problems."

"I don't know," I said. "We don't want to get in trouble."

"I promise you," he said, "no problems."

"Will you go swimming with us?" I asked.

"Oh, yes," he said and walked off.

Two minutes later he returned wearing only boxers.

I turned to Dennis and said, "I guess we're going swimming now."

Right in the middle of daylight.

Dennis told me to enter the water first. "Go for it," he said. I thought the sunlight might have warmed the temperature. No such luck. The water was just as bone chilling as our nighttime swims.

I was easing my way in when out of nowhere the brother cannonballed off a ledge and landed right next to me, covering me in freezing water. I figured I might as well jump in and get it over with. Dennis followed. We laughed and splashed. This wasn't one of our quiet, covert, nightly swims. This was overt, and it was working.

"Just don't swim and touch the other side, because the Taliban will see it and come get my daughters. So, don't touch the other side."

"Okay, I promise," I said. "I won't touch the other side." We kept our word.

We continued to swim and splash around in the water. The brother thought we were having a fun time playing, but we were secretly and quickly working.

I dropped a stick in the water and counted three seconds before it traveled a yard from north to south. From shore to shore, the river measured 104 yards. At its deepest, the river was about ten feet, and the gradients on the entries were gradual. Water temperature was cold but doable for a short crossing, but the family would need to immediately change into dry clothes once across the river and then be hurried to a waiting vehicle and given warm liquids. The soil composition was silt-like sand, so footing would present few problems beyond the occasional slippery rock. The entrance side of the river had minimal large rocks but still was sufficient for anchoring a safety line. That side also was sparser in vegetation, but a few small trees could serve as cover and concealment. Upon closer inspection, the waist-high rock wall was confirmed as ideal cover for the family.

At one point, we were close to the edge of the far side when two motorcycles drove past, a driver and passenger on each.

"Those guys are Taliban," our host informed us. "They are scouts, and they drive back and forth all day."

The next time one of the motorcycles drove by, we waved to the Taliban thirty yards from us. They waved back!

The sun was starting to go down when we completed our work, so we swam to the bank on our hosts' property and changed into dry clothes.

The four of us—Nakita and Sasha had stayed safe, dry, and warm while we were in the river—walked with Islamadad and his brother back through their farm. We spent some time thanking the brothers and the family for their kindness, handed them some money for their time and hospitality, and said our goodbyes. But that didn't mean we wouldn't be back to use their property for a crossing later that night.

As our group walked back toward the road and the hostel, Dennis and I assessed the situation.

The farm property was exactly what we needed as an exit point. An unfortunate part of war is that innocents sometimes get caught up in the middle, but we didn't want to do anything to endanger the family that we didn't have to do, especially the daughters. Every human life is valuable, and these were especially good people. We had a responsibility to consider everyone's safety with any decisions we made.

"What if this guy comes out of his house in the middle of the night while we are moving people through his property?" Dennis asked.

"We'll have to zip-tie him and tie him to a tree. Tape his mouth," I said. "His family will find him in the morning."

"There could even be a situation where we'd have to kill him," Dennis added.

I knew Dennis's last comment was his dark humor. Especially in our part of the military community, such comments tended to lighten the mood of tense times before or after dangerous operations. The more dangerous the operation, the worse the humor, it seemed. But Sasha wasn't in the military. She was a nurse.

For the first time since Sasha joined us, she showed signs of uneasiness. I told her we were just joking about killing the man. But once fear is sparked in someone, it takes root like cancer.

Eighteen

───── ★ ─────

Heartbreak Among Success

WE HAD OUR CROSSING LOCATION SECURED. ALL WE NEEDED was the family to rescue.

After leaving the farm, our team reassembled, loaded up our gear, and made a cave with our backpacks and gear in the rear of the SUV for hiding the family. We drove twenty miles to a restaurant of sorts, making notes along the way where we saw military personnel, their demeanor, and discernible patterns. Our plan was to remain at the restaurant until nautical twilight, when both the horizon and the brightest stars were visible, and then leave to meet the family at the crossing point.

While we waited, Jake abruptly informed us he was no longer comfortable being part of our operation and that he had hired a taxi to take him back to Dushanbe. We still had Sasha, who could speak Tajik and Russian, to help with interpretation if needed.

A short time after Jake left, he contacted us to let us know he and his driver had passed a forty-six-vehicle convoy of Russian BTR-82 armored personnel carriers, armored vehicles, and troop carriers, which we immediately passed on to a contact at a US government agency.

About 9 p.m. we returned to the SUVs and headed back to our hostel to stage for the operation. Even though our cell service was off, every time our phones were on, our cell service turned on.

Our communications had been hacked.

We started receiving a barrage of calls from Russian numbers. If we received three calls in a row from different locations, we knew we were triangulated, meaning the Russians likely knew our exact location and were tracking us. We made the decision to completely shut off all electronics.

We also noticed a much heavier military presence along our drive than on the way to the restaurant. When we arrived at the hostel, we observed a small, unidentifiable military squad that hadn't been there before.

That's when Sasha got spooked and said she also wanted to leave. She had appeared uneasy since hearing the conversation between Dennis and me. I understood. I think the idea of rescuing the family had sounded cool and noble to Sasha in theory, and I knew that as a nurse she especially wanted to help the pregnant woman. But the intensity grew to more than she had expected.

"No hard feelings," I told her. "We'll make sure you get safely to where you need to go."

Then I pulled Nakita off to the side.

"Hey, look," I said. "It's just you, me, Dennis, and the drivers now. I don't expect you to do this. You've already done enough and risked your life by being with us all week. No hard feelings if you don't want to do this either. I'm not going to pressure you into putting your life at risk any further."

Without hesitating, she responded, "You guys can't do this without me. You need me. I've already started this, and I'm staying with you. If you have to hide a body, I'm all in." Not all heroes wear capes or military uniforms. Nakita is a real one, a selfless soul willing to risk everything for a stranger she never met. She knew this could be her final hours. We could all feel the level of risk increasing by the minute with rescuing this family. These past few months had revealed a few heroes like Nakita, and they also had exposed the cowards in governments around the world who were willfully allowing this to happen, those so-called journalists who choose to be silent, and the many others who could act but didn't. I was proud of Nakita.

Despite things deteriorating, Dennis and I decided to continue on with the rescue. The family had traveled for days and was desperate and counting on us. We had to be there for them. However, as we prepared to leave the hostel, one of the drivers balked and called his boss. When the call ended, he appeared to give a short update to the other driver.

"We are going home," he said. "We don't want to be here anymore."

"You can't leave now," I said. "How much money would it take for you guys to stay?"

"You could give me a million dollars," he replied, "but I cannot spend it if I am dead."

Not only would they not continue the operation with us, he added, but they also wouldn't even drive us back to Dushanbe. They were done with us.

Our planned rescue was now crumbling.

Dennis got back in touch with Matt Nelson and requested immediate support for new drivers.

"The soonest we can get them to you is in a day or two," Matt responded.

Even by the next morning wouldn't be soon enough. With no drivers, we had no choice but to abort the operation. My heart broke, and I couldn't even process that the attempt to rescue the family had ended. Although a rescue was not our primary mission for being there, my heart had become invested in helping this family as we communicated with them, moved them, and staged their rescue.

The family waited for us just across the river, hidden behind the rock wall the entire time. I couldn't get rid of the thought of the pregnant woman and the child lying out in the cold all night. They had made it through more than a dozen Taliban checkpoints between Kabul and the border to reach the final step. But while only shouting distance away, we could not get to them. Even if we could have, we could not responsibly bring them across with no ride out.

We arranged for a ride to pick up the family and transport them back to Kabul so the mother could deliver her baby in a hospital there. Hopefully, the family could make another attempt to leave Afghanistan.

I felt sick and angry. It was the same anger I had felt so many times years ago in these same mountains of Afghanistan. It was the type of disgust and anger that can come only from seeing the unspeakable horrors of evil first-hand. I had to shift focus back to Dennis and the crew.

"You are not leaving us here," I told the drivers. "Just take us to a different place to spend tonight."

Dennis and I made it pretty clear we were not negotiating. The drivers agreed to take us, and the six of us left the staging area.

At our new location, a home of a trusted local, we turned one phone on. The incoming calls started back immediately. We turned the phone off and worked to get a satellite phone signal.

Dennis called the government agency official back in the United States to report our status.

"Shut your phones off and conduct your E&E plan immediately," she said. "Do whatever it takes to get off the border and back to Dushanbe."

Nakita and Sasha were better off separated from us in the event we became compromised, and Nakita knew of a safe camp to the east they could go to. I paid one of the drivers to take them there.

The other driver made good on his threat to leave us and, when we weren't watching, disappeared.

It was one o'clock in the morning. The owner of the home contacted a new driver to take us to Dushanbe. We made sure he understood that we needed the most trusted person he knew with a safe vehicle and all the proper paperwork.

"I'll pay five hundred US dollars, but I want to leave right now," I said. "No questions asked."

"I've got the perfect driver for you," he assured.

Thirty minutes later, a smiling man in his midtwenties showed up driving a Toyota Corolla. He knew not a syllable of English. I snapped a photo and sent it to our government contact for a rapid facial recognition check. Dennis also sent a picture of Nakita and Sasha with their driver.

At 2 a.m., we said quick goodbyes to Nakita and Sasha and hopped in the car for the long drive to Dushanbe. I thought we were saying goodbye to Nakita.

"I am going to keep going east up the river," she said. Each step along the way, she supplied us with crossing points with grid coordinates and pictures. Nakita was committed to the end.

Driving Us Crazy

No sooner were Dennis and I on our way back to Dushanbe than the driver popped open an energy drink. Then he placed some kind of substance on the back of his hand—it looked like hashish—and started snorting it. We made awkward eye contact. The silence and the stare were broken by a crazy laugh and him grabbing the steering wheel as if gearing up at the starting line of the Daytona 500.

His car had no seat belts, and we were driving on dangerous mountain roads with steep cliffs on the sides. Dennis and I hadn't slept in forever, and we both were in a state of indecision as to whether we should sleep or stay awake to monitor the driver.

I wound up drifting off to sleep and then waking up to sudden jerks on the steering wheel. Once, I woke up to see headlights coming almost directly at us before we veered back to our side of the road. The driver slapped his face a few times as if to wake himself up.

Sleeping was not the wisest choice and might sound impossible after the recent failed rescue. But after days of no sleep, our minds and bodies were quitting, and in the surprising calmness of our crazy driver's drug-induced shenanigans, we couldn't help but drift off. What could we do, anyway, to stop us from driving off a cliff or heading into an oncoming vehicle? It probably would be better not to see death coming.

Two and a half hours into the trip, still driving through the mountains, the Corolla began to overheat, and our driver shut off the engine. Right in the middle of the road.

Dennis and I exited the car. I first looked for a place we could run to for escape if necessary. Then we removed our backpacks from the car and laid them on the ground at the start of the escape path I had mentally plotted. My aching groin injury had held up during the trip, although I didn't know how much horsepower I had left in me. But I was prepared to hightail at top possible speed if any unfriendlies drove upon us.

The driver opened the hood and waved steam out of his face. The engine coolant tank was empty. We poured in all our drinking water, but that was not enough. The driver started tinkering with parts under the hood even though the problem had been clearly identified. In Dari, I tried to suggest we push the car to the side of the road, but my Dari wasn't translating well. Finally, we put together enough hand signals and gestures to convince him we should move the car. The three of us pushed the Corolla to the side, and then the driver resumed trying to fix problems under the hood that didn't exist.

I also tried to tell the driver of a way we could put more fluids in the radiator, but he wasn't understanding my attempts at demonstrating how each of us could pee into the coolant tank. After an hour of failed communications and needless pulling and pushing and banging of engine parts, a big rig truck came up the road and pulled up beside us. Two Afghan men were inside, and they talked with our driver. They just happened to have bottles of water in their truck and filled the coolant tank and got the Corolla started back up. There is evil in every part of the world, but, fortunately, I have found it to be overshadowed by the hospitality of good people. While the Afghanistan region is home to a *lot* of evil, there are still many people there whose hearts are good and whose charity gives us hope for their future and ours.

Surprisingly surviving the trip, we made it back to Dushanbe. Flights out of Dushanbe were not daily, with usually two options per week. We would spend the next couple of days in our motel rooms writing up our route and fording reports. If you've read how boring military-style reports are, you should experience how boring they are to write. They're all data points, and writing them proved especially a struggle on not even ten hours of sleep over the previous week. But Dennis and I had both done this plenty times before, and we got to it.

But, of course, some other opportunity always seemed to arise for us.

We were invited to a birthday dinner for Dave Eubank. Among the guests was the Navy SEAL corpsman who had told us the Panj River would be too cold for us to swim in. I made sure he could see that we had somehow managed to survive, and even rubbed in my point by showing him a video clip of us treading water.

"Oh, yeah, but you guys are studs," he said. "I meant anybody else getting in, the water would have been too cold."

I corrected him. "You said the water was too cold for anybody to be in and that it was impossible to cross."

He awkwardly chuckled, and I moved on, point delivered. He was a really good guy, so it was all in fun, but I had to rub it in. I appreciated him in any case. Corpsmen are always trying to play it safe medically and have probably saved me from my recklessness more than once.

A Stomach for the Job

Following up on a conversation Dennis and I had with Dave that night, Dave later sent a text introducing us to the number two man under the resistance fighters' leader, Ahmad Massoud, who was helping move vulnerable people across the border and needing support for his resistance fighters. As bad as we might have wanted to, we knew we couldn't help the resistance fighters. But we did want to see how we could support in any humanitarian aid.

Ahmad was the oldest son of Ahmad Shah Massoud, an Afghan rebel commander in the anti-Soviet resistance of the 1980s. In the nineties, Massoud was the top commander of the opposition against the Taliban until he was assassinated in a suicide bombing on September 9, 2001—two days before the 9/11 attacks.

Massoud led the Northern Alliance, and Osama bin Laden led the Taliban. After the Soviets withdrew from Afghanistan, a tribal war broke out between them. Even while the Taliban was in power, Massoud and the Northern Alliance continued to fight. Two days before the attacks on the World Trade

Center and the Pentagon, two al-Qaeda members posing as journalists met Massoud for what was supposed to be an interview. One was wearing a suicide bomb vest that he detonated.

Bin Laden had brilliantly ordered the hit because he realized the United States would go after him following the attacks on our nation, and Massoud would be an ally we could align with in fighting against the Taliban. Massoud's assassination struck fear in resistance fighters, and many jumped over to the Taliban. When the United States went into Afghanistan because of 9/11, the Northern Alliance had already been fractured, although many of those who became our allies and interpreters and built the ANA were from Massoud's Northern Alliance.

Now the son, Ahmad, had risen to lead the anti-Taliban resistance fighters in the remote Panjshir Valley, less than one hundred miles north of Kabul. That area has long held off occupation attempts by foreign countries, including the British Empire in the nineteenth century and the Soviet Union in the eighties. Ahmad's National Resistance Front had rebuffed the Taliban, too, when it was in power from 1996 to 2001. And even in the days after Kabul fell during the US withdrawal, the Panjshir Valley remained the one part of Afghanistan the Taliban had yet to overtake.

"I would prefer to die than to surrender," Ahmad had said. "I'm the son of Ahmad Shah Massoud. Surrender is not a word in my vocabulary."[1]

Ahmad's number two man, "Fattah," wanted to talk about ways we could provide support to the resistance fighters as well as request information from us for helping people cross from Afghanistan into Tajikistan.

Dennis and I agreed to meet with Fattah in Dushanbe but had to ensure he was not being followed. After days of operating within eyesight of the Taliban and the Tajik, Russian, and Chinese militaries, our biggest threat at the motel was Tajik police raiding our rooms while we typed reports. The break from the unrelenting stress was rather enjoyable, and we didn't want to ruin what we had by unknowingly leading someone to our motel.

We needed to set up a surveillance detection route (SDR) that would reveal if Fattah was being tailed. Without revealing our method, an SDR might look like arranging for Fattah to meet Dennis at a restaurant at a specific time. When Fattah arrived, Dennis would meet him on the street corner and say, "Actually, Chad can't make it here on time, so he is going to meet us at this restaurant instead." By dragging Fattah to the second location, I would be able to run surveillance for anyone following him. Or, I could even spot surveillance on their meeting location by identifying a surveillance vantage point and observing suspicious activity. Then I would show up at the new meeting site to join Dennis and Fattah.

Dennis and I walked the location of the meeting point the day before, scouted the location, and set up good SDR positions and a lane to pass Fattah through. The day of the meeting, I arrived two hours ahead of time to secure a good vantage point for the first meeting. I found one at a restaurant across the street.

I ordered breakfast and sent Dennis pictures of me drinking tea while I waited for my food. Then, knowing he hadn't eaten yet, I sent him pictures of my delicious Tajik meal. After I finished my meal, Fattah had yet to show. The longer I remained at the restaurant with my meal completed, the more suspicious I would look. While Fattah seemed to be taking forever, I was trying to come up with a plan when a small group of men entered the restaurant and looked around for an open table. I thought it was better for me to look like I had company than to sit alone. I caught their attention and waved them over to sit with me, an appropriate custom in Tajik culture. They appreciated the offer and joined me.

"Can I get you anything?" I asked.

"We are going to get some yogurt," one said.

"I'll get one too," I said, even though I was stuffed from my meal.

Drinking a glass of yogurt might sound terrible, especially when you see how thick and clumpy the yogurt is. It's surprisingly tasty, tart with a little salt added. Aziz and my old Afghan teammates would drink yogurt especially when the weather turned hot. They claimed the yogurt cooled them off. Like they always say, there's nothing like choking down a warm, clumpy glass of yogurt on a hot summer day.

I ordered glasses of yogurt for the table.

As we enjoyed drinking our yogurts, I said I wanted to take a picture of us. I held up my phone camera and counted, "One, two, three." Instead of "Cheers!" the men said in unison, "Vodka!" Russia certainly had its influence on the culture.

I texted the picture to Dennis with the line, "I met some new friends. One, two, three . . . Vodka!"

"Unbelievable," Dennis texted back.

Fattah finally showed up, and Dennis stalled him so I could surveil the vantage point and discreetly snap pictures with my phone. Then Dennis and Fattah left, with Dennis dragging him through our SDR lane to the second location. Once I was sure that Fattah was not being followed, I joined them for yet another lunch—not an easy assignment after a huge breakfast and a glass of yogurt. Dennis enjoyed his turn to laugh. The Turkish pizza was so good, though, that I didn't pause to stuff it inside me. Technically, I was on vacation. Kind of.

Fattah told us they were hiding Afghan families in safe houses and the mountains, and they needed information from our fording and route recons to navigate women and children across the river border to safety. He also asked for help getting supplies for the resistance fighters: cold weather gear, medical supplies, weapons and ammunition . . . *and* explosives and rockets, optics and night vision, helicopters, and bombs for an aircraft he had acquired. Cold weather gear and medicine were humanitarian aid, which we could provide. Helping with the rest of his list was off-limits for us. Fighter to fighter and as common enemies of the Taliban, I would have loved to help. But we could not break laws and freely continue our mission to help the Afghan people.

Worth the Risk

Providing that lifesaving data directly into the hands of the people who needed it was the purpose of our mission. Being able to distribute it brought a sense of achievement and victory because the data would result in saving innocent human lives.

As we left Tajikistan, it still was difficult to think about not getting that family across the river to safety. Could I have done something different to help them? Because the man was a commando, he was a prime Taliban target. To this day, I do not know the family's status beyond their safe return to Kabul. I might never know and will always wonder.

I've had to remind myself that our mission was to provide good reports that could be used to rescue people from Afghanistan. As a former Force Recon Marine, I see information and data as people. When I entered a battlefield to do a route or fording site report for Marines, or compiled a reconnaissance report for bridge crossings, or created a spot report detailing the location and actions of bad guys, the words and numbers on the pages were all about keeping people alive.

Dennis and I shared our reports with government agencies and other NGO groups. We know that the routes we mapped and data we collected have successfully delivered people to freedom and saved human lives. Our mission was a tremendous success and one I will always be proud to have been a part of. I have heard comments from within the NGO community that Dennis and I were reckless, cowboyish, and crazy for going out there. Perhaps those critics are correct. But we did what we believed in our hearts had to be done. We never were naive to the risks, but we concluded the end result was worth the risk, even if just one family made it to freedom, or one little girl was spared from a life of rape or slavery, or if one little boy avoided being indoctrinated into the Taliban's Sharia and becoming an evil terrorist. Yes, what we did might have been crazy. But it was worth it.

Note: Dennis has been nominated for the Navy and Marine Corps Medal for his courage and actions by putting his own life in grave danger in order to save human life during the Afghan border reconnaissance operation. The medal is the highest noncombat decoration awarded for heroism by the United States Department of the Navy to members of the United States Navy and United States Marine Corps.

Nineteen

— ★ —

The Journey Ahead

WE LIVE IN A DIFFERENT WORLD THAN THE ONE WE WOKE up to on April 14, 2021—the day President Biden announced the United States would withdraw all our troops from Afghanistan.

It's not hubris when we Americans consider ourselves the leader of the free world. It's not exaggeration to call whoever occupies the Oval Office the most powerful person in the world. What we do as a country and the policies and decisions of our president carry a global impact.

The United States lost, Afghans lost, and much of the world lost when we pulled our military out of Afghanistan. The world is not as safe as it was on that day. To be determined is whether the balance of power among the world's nations will shift as a result.

Afghanistan has been damned for recorded history to be a major player in great power competitions and has been known as the graveyard of their ambitions since Alexander the Great. It finds itself in such a position because it occupies a central location on the major strategic crossroads from the Middle East to Asia and between great powers such as ancient Greece, Byzantium, Persia, Russia, China, and India. Indeed, well over a century ago, the great American strategist Alfred Thayer Mahan wrote a book in which he described the importance of Afghanistan (*The Problem of Asia*) and coined the term *Near East*, which the State Department still uses for a whole bureau to this day.

Two countries stand to gain the most from our departure: China and Iran. The forty-seven-mile border China shares with Afghanistan could become forty-seven of the most important miles on the world map.

China imports more oil than any other country. Iran is rich in oil, but its sale of crude is a perpetual target for economic sanctions. As the country between China and Iran, Afghanistan offers a land connection for China to obtain oil from Iran without detection. Additionally, any prospective Iran–China oil pipeline through Afghanistan should be considered in the context of serving as an alternative to the sea routes that China presently uses to import its oil from the Middle East. Similarly, our vacancy from Afghanistan diminishes our ability to sever highway systems being built by the Chinese along the Wakhan Corridor.[1] These factors will complicate our ability to restrict Chinese oil importation and Chinese ground-based trade at a time of crisis. It is notable that our absence from Afghanistan also helps China surround India by forming a direct land connection with Pakistan and significantly adds to China's penetration of Central Asia with its borders on Tajikistan, Uzbekistan, and so on.

Afghanistan also is a mineral-rich land, with estimates of $1–3 trillion in natural resources. The untapped resources include significant amounts of lithium, which is a key ingredient in the batteries that power electric cars and home power units. However, far beyond lithium, Afghanistan is blessed with an abundance of rare earth minerals and other critical materials with applications for technologies not yet invented. China has cornered the global market on the sourcing and sale of these minerals and materials. We owned the resources in Afghanistan but allowed the Chinese to buy rights to the land we were protecting. Now we have increased China's control over a colossal supply of these materials for the tech race over the next hundred years.

Then there's the question of what becomes of Bagram Air Base, which I and many military strategists consider potentially one of the most strategic military locations in the world with its position between Iraq, Iran, Russia, and China. Our enemies would covet controlling the global stronghold that we forfeited for no explainable reason.

I've made appearances on national and global media outlets concerning Afghanistan since the president's withdrawal announcement. When I was on an Israeli national media outlet, they had serious concerns about how America's departure from Afghanistan would impact Israel. Afghanistan will become a place where terrorism grows. Education in the madrasas (Islamic colleges) will include the systematic deep-seated anti-Semitism inherent in Sharia and the dedicated training of new jihadi cadres to hate the West and the Jewish people, particularly the Jewish state of Israel. If Iran's nuclear program grows because of its relationship with China, Iran becomes a greater threat to Israel. From the Israeli perspective, the dominos have already started falling from a national security standpoint, and they have every right to be concerned about finding the ultimate results of Afghanistan's fall on their doorstep.

Less obvious dominos in the region are falling related to China, Iran, Turkey, Pakistan, and India. For example, in response to the Iranian and Turkish economic collapses, China has propped them up with funding and essentially has begun turning them into its geopolitical minions. In that context, the danger Iran poses to our interests in Afghanistan is clear. But more obscure is the threat Turkey poses to our interests. Afghanistan represents a fulcrum of sorts in the competition between India and Pakistan. Afghanistan has a historical affinity with Indian culture, but its religion draws it to Pakistan, so its identity is torn and up for grabs. The deepening ties between Turkish president Recep Tayyip Erdoğan and Pakistan's Imran Khan have led to a situation where China, through Turkey, is employing its Islamic outreach not only to destabilize Indian Muslim populations but to create an Islamic axis from Ankara to Islamabad, which runs through Afghanistan. Few people are taking note that Erdoğan has a very aggressive Indian strategy to destabilize the Indian subcontinent and assert Turkish leadership as the standard-bearer for Islam—something which he then seeks to leverage in all his other conflicts in North Africa, Israel, Cyprus and Greece, the Balkans, and even in Europe over its expatriate Muslims. That means what happens in Kabul will have a far-reaching impact in many places. That makes Afghanistan a critical strategic battleground between India and Pakistan as well as between the Gulf Arab states, such as the UAE, Saudi Arabia, and Turkey. Moreover, if one can imagine a day after the Ayatollah's regime in Tehran goes away, then India's cultural affinity with Iran raises the prospect of an Iranian–Pakistani competition over Afghanistan that reflects the larger Indian–Turkish alignment.

The United States' national security also has been compromised, because it was in our best interest to keep the Taliban at bay. The human intelligence network we built up over twenty years thwarted planned terrorist attacks at home and in foreign countries on a scale we will never know. Our intelligence network's tentacles spread throughout Afghanistan and into Pakistan. Now, that network is suddenly gone. How long would it take to rebuild the network that, essentially, we gave up overnight? Obviously, twenty years!

I pray my prediction is wrong, but I anticipate the United States will suffer another major terror attack inside our nation as a result of allowing unvetted people into our country during the evacuations and embracing open borders while a hotbed of terrorism has been given a new home with no global intervention. When such an attack occurs, I anticipate the US government and mainstream media will blame the NGOs. But, again, I want to say we NGOs were under stringent demands to vet every person we evacuated, and not one of them will make it here without the State Department's approval. NGOs do not have that ability, power, or authority. Unfortunately, our government was responsible for rushing unvetted people onto planes to boost the number of people it evacuated.

We also let the world down. The British, Germans, and other allied nations had significant numbers of troops in Afghanistan, but our military was the recognized leader. The United Nations and NATO don't take the lead; we do. As the world leader, taking the lead is our responsibility. In abandoning our allies, we abandoned our responsibility to Afghanistan and to the world.

In the process, our country has lost respect. We have been a country that others counted on to do the right thing. In Afghanistan, we didn't. The lack of foreign political leaders who voiced support for our withdrawal was deafening. Their silence clearly said that America did the wrong thing strategically, economically, and morally. How could any country trust us again in future conflicts in which we engage? The truth is they can't, and we have a long road ahead of us to earn back their trust.

As for Afghanistan, I'm afraid the country will once again fall into civil war, just as it did after the Russian withdrawal. It is difficult to say it actually hasn't been in a multisided civil war since the onset of the withdrawal. The inaccurate reports that resistance fighters are lacking the will to defend their country has caused an underestimation of their ability and determination. Many of the commandos presently in the Panjshir Valley received US Army Special Forces training. Ahmad Massoud is building up the resistance to take on the Taliban. He has fighters who remained in the country for that purpose. Others left to get their families to safety and then returned to fight for their homeland. Also, we cannot overlook the history of the Taliban and groups like them. It's inevitable that they will splinter and fight one another for power, control, and territory because they are not capable of unification or governing people and a nation.

The X factor in a civil war is which side the United States will back. The Taliban has the support of Pakistan and Iran, and a civil war would disrupt China's intentions in Afghanistan. Unfortunately, our political leaders' vote is cast. Our government negotiated with the Taliban instead of the legitimate Afghan government. Our political leaders pulled the military support that had supported the Afghan government for twenty years. The United States decided to back the Taliban, and it is unforeseeable how that could be undone.

Little Hope for SIVs

After the fall of Kabul and the Taliban gaining control, SIV applicants and their family members who remained in Afghanistan were in danger and continue to be. During the NCS deputies' August 14 committee meeting, they concluded that SIV applicants who are post–chief of mission approval and have approved I-360 petitions would be priority, but only 1,052 applicants met the criteria of the 17,469 who were still in the SIV pipeline.

The US withdrawal and abandonment of our allies created a surge in SIV applicants who are desperate for rescue and live in fear of death every day. I receive messages daily begging for help. My family also receives them, as does anyone associated with me publicly, because people believe if they can reach me somehow, we can do something. The messages are heartbreaking, every single one. We receive pictures and videos of people beaten. Yesterday I got a voice message from an SIV applicant crying hysterically and begging for me to do anything because the Taliban was outside his home and they were going to kill him and his family for working with Americans.

From August to December 2021 the SIV pipeline has increased 100 percent and now has over thirty-five thousand applicants. It is uncertain where each individual case is in the State Department's complex fourteen-step process, how long it will take to complete, or if there is even a plan to evacuate those who are still in Afghanistan. How could we at this point? I am thankful for those we have moved to lily pads like Abu Dhabi; at least we know they are safe and have a chance.

A Welcomed People

The State Department continues to update Save Our Allies and other NGOs through nightly conference calls. In addition to staying apprised of the situation in Afghanistan, we also can know when rules and policies are changing so we continue to operate within legal requirements. The calls have been helpful, and I appreciate the State Department's openness and commitment to communicating with us.

In mid-December 2021, the State Department said fewer than a dozen American citizens who wanted to leave—there's that phrase again—and had the necessary documents remained in Afghanistan. At the same time, we were in contact with a group of fifty-seven and a group of forty-five US blue passport holders who were trying to leave and had contacted the State Department but were not receiving return communications. I believe more like two thousand Americans were trying to get out of Afghanistan when that figure was released.

The rescue requests are still coming in. We expect evacuations will continue, although on a gradual decline, into 2024. Resettlement of refugees could last a decade. That is one reason why Sarah and I created Save Our Allies as a separate organization from our other foundations. Save Our Allies' work will continue as long as needed.

Through our work in US humanitarian centers, we ensure refugees are treated with dignity and respect through the transition process. When Afghans left their homes to evacuate, we advised them to each pack their backpack with everything it could hold. That's all the possessions they were able to bring with them. Sometimes the military had to tell them to leave their backpack behind. In those cases, the people arrive here with only the documents in their hands.

They lost everything and are completely starting over.

Imagine today, with no notice, that you were told to fill a backpack and leave, and you would never see any possessions, your home, or your neighbors again. You would be moving into the unknown with nothing. That's what they face, and on top of so much loss.

For some Afghans who want to hold on to more of their culture and traditions, living in a culture closer to theirs than the United States offers the best for them. I expect the UAE and Qatar will accept many of those. But I have no doubt that those who want to move here and assimilate into Western culture will make positive contributions to our country.

For the refugees coming to America, we will help them acclimate into our society so they will not feel like foreigners in their new homes.

As a whole, Afghans are kind, humble, giving, and compassionate family people. They are not the Taliban. They are the good ones escaping the Taliban. They come from a culture that values hard work. A member of the royal family told us the UAE had four hundred thousand Afghans living in their country and would gladly accept more because of the Afghans' dedication to working hard when they assimilated into the UAE economy. I have no doubt American companies will acquire great employees and smart entrepreneurs will emerge from among the refugees. They possess an ability to figure things out in a business sense and will prove to be job creators for America.

Afghans also tend to be community-oriented, which provides a tremendous opportunity for the American Christian church to embrace them. Judeo-Christian principles resonate with Afghans, even though they live in a predominantly Muslim culture. They will have the option of attending mosques in America, but their newfound freedom of religion also will allow them to explore spiritual truths for themselves. I expect many will discover Christianity and other beliefs here. That excites me!

A Community in Need of Healing

Our Mighty Oaks Foundation is already planning for new opportunities.

Over the past ten years, over 4,500 military warriors and spouses have entered our recovery program, and I have spoken about resiliency to over 400,000 active-duty troops. I speak to two active units a month, so I am in constant contact with our service members, ranging from the seventeen-year-old recruit at boot camp up to senior enlisted personnel and officers all over the world.

In private moments, many open up to me about their personal struggles. They tell me our military is in bad shape. The level of motivation has plummeted. Distrust of the federal government has skyrocketed. Many disagree with the decisions coming from our highest government leaders.

Perhaps the military has been at this place in our nation's history before, but in my thirty years of serving in and working with the military, I have never seen morale this low.

From my observations, morale started sinking because of COVID-19. Training was being shut down because of the pandemic, and over recent years units are being monitored for their coronavirus infection rates. Commanders' level of success for unit readiness became based on how few cases showed up in the unit. To keep case numbers down, our troops often were prevented from going on leave or traveling home. Case count was an unfair metric.

Then vaccine mandates became an issue because commanders were essentially placed in competition against each other to see who could achieve 100 percent vaccination rates. The number of COVID-19 cases and vaccines administered became more important than training and combat readiness. Service members are being discharged for refusing to take the vaccine without regard to valid religious and medical exemptions, in the process losing their benefits, retirements, ability to serve their nation, and the dignity of an honorable discharge. All this was taking place while, during the third quarter of 2021, more service members died by suicide than from coronavirus.[2]

The Afghanistan withdrawal was the final blow for many in the military.

A longtime friend who is approaching thirty years in the Marines, all in special operations and with multiple awards for combat valor, told me after the withdrawal, "I am embarrassed to put on a uniform. This country is over."

I don't agree that our country is done as we know it, but I understand his frustration. I felt it. Based on my travels and conversations with service members from across the spectrum, my friend's perception is systemic throughout the military.

Whether or not we want to hear it or believe it in America, it's the hard truth about what's going on among our active military. To me, the morale, the willingness to serve, and the lack of confidence in top leadership ranks all the way up to the commander in chief poses a national security risk. We must have good morale and warriors who are willing to serve America and our interests around the world. Without our troops there is no America, and without America there is no free world.

Because Mighty Oaks is a ministry to the military and veteran community, I also am seeing a widespread negative impact from the withdrawal among veterans—especially those who served in Afghanistan.

I still deal with life and death every day because the veterans served by Mighty Oaks are at high risk for suicide. Adjusting for age and sex differences, the suicide rate among veterans was 53.2 percent higher than for nonveteran US adults according to the most recent reports. The US Department of Veteran Affairs' report on veteran suicide prevention found that in 2019 an average of 17.2 veterans died by suicide per day. Surprisingly, that is on a downward trend from 22 a day in 2014 and 20 in 2017, all based on a lot of work from the Veteran Service Organizations community and organizations like Mighty Oaks. If the next round of reports are honest, I am certain, based on what we are seeing on the ground level, that those numbers will horrifically trend in the opposite direction, leaving a wake of destruction in the military community.

At Mighty Oaks, we are dealing with a significant increase in suicide ideations and suicide attempts. Going back to the completion of the withdrawal, we have received more calls for help and applications for our programs than at any other time in our history. In 2021, the national suicide hotline call volume increased over 1,000 percent. In addition to a surge from Afghanistan veterans, we are working with more Iraqi veterans because the Afghanistan withdrawal has reminded them of the hasty Iraq withdrawal in 2011.

The consensus among the military members and veterans we help is that the United States has betrayed our integrity and failed to keep our word to our allies. They are questioning whether other countries still respect us and will support us in future wars. They're asking how our military could ever become involved in another war again and if we'll regain support for our military from within our own country.

Then there are the deeply personal questions that are crushing to hear.

"Does my service even count?"

"Was my service for nothing?"

"I lost my legs—for what?"

"I lost my buddy—for what?"

"What did my son die for?"

A September 2021 survey by Blue Star Families found that 78 percent of veterans who served in Afghanistan believed the United States had an obligation to help Afghan allies. Also, 46 percent had taken action to help Afghan allies through a donation, volunteering, or sharing information.[3]

We've heard some of those stories.

"I was talking with my interpreter on the phone."

"I was trying to help them get into the airport through Google Earth."

"I was on the phone with him. Then I heard gunshots, and his phone went dead."

Stories of buddies lost. Or still there and unable to get out. Or no longer making contact and feared captured or dead.

On the first Veterans Day after the withdrawal, a close friend who's a retired Navy SEAL told me, "This feels like the most hollow, fake holiday ever in my life. I feel like my entire time as a SEAL was a lie. Like it was all for nothing. I believed something that just wasn't true about this country."

Our military, current and past, is a hurting community.

At Mighty Oaks, my team and I are doing everything in our power to help them heal from the pain.

We also are creating a program for interpreters who come to the United States, because as they integrate into American society and things finally slow down for them, the horrors of war they experienced over twenty years are going to surface. They'll need a place to go for healing and to learn how to acclimate to their new normal.

My next personal mission is to be there to help these two groups heal, because that's the burden God has placed heavy on my heart moving ahead.

Twenty

— ★ —

The Calling Continues

THIS EXPERIENCE HAS BEEN A TIME OF LEARNING FOR me too.

I've observed how politics is both important and unimportant.

As the saying goes, elections have consequences. We tend to focus on selfish results, like higher gas prices or higher taxes. But how we vote can cost people their lives, and I understand even more so now why Aziz and his family cared so much about the US presidential results at their Kabul election party in 2004.

I've learned the importance of speaking out more, even when doing so is unpopular, because we have allowed the truth to go untold—or falsehoods to be told—for so long that something like the Afghanistan debacle could be pulled off. I can't help but believe that if Americans had known more of the truth about what we were doing in Afghanistan, why it was important globally and from a national security standpoint, and what the Afghan people were like, the debacle would not have been allowed to happen. Elections have consequences, and so does keeping the truth from people. This book is not and was never intended to be a partisan attack on a political party or an administration; it is simply my attempt to tell the truth so the world will know it and so you can come to your own conclusions as we shape our future in this world together.

But I also have seen how politics don't matter. People have come together regardless of political affiliation or who they voted for. Whether they went there in person, provided financial support, contacted political leaders, shared names of people needing rescue, or prayed, Americans and our neighbors around the world have come together in a united quest to do the right thing in response to the need for our fellow humans in Afghanistan. Despite my frustrations, anger, confusion, and all the other emotions I've felt since the spring of 2021, this common ground from which many of us have worked is most encouraging to me.

Another lesson we can learn from Afghanistan is the danger of political correctness. If America wants to win the war on terror, we must treat it seriously because it is serious. We must be willing to know and name our enemy. Throughout the war, people who used the term *radical Islamic terrorists* to describe the enemy were often criticized for being bigots or using "hate speech" when, in fact, these adversaries of freedom were radical, were Islamic, and were using violence and terror against us. Over time, due to so many leaders prioritizing political correctness over truth, even the term *terrorism* was replaced with *violent extremism*.

The truth is that the Taliban and their terrorist allies don't call themselves violent extremists or even terrorists. They call themselves jihadists. They are a danger to America and our allies because they follow and seek to impose on others Sharia—divine Islamic law. Our allies, like Aziz and others in the Muslim community, recognized this and not only spoke out against it but fought it alongside us for twenty years. They have no desire to live under Sharia, because it calls for the sorts of brutal violence and oppression we see in the actions of the Taliban, ISIS, al-Qaeda, and every other violent jihadist group worldwide.

The reality is there are millions of good Muslim people in Afghanistan right now who are the victims of the Taliban's jihad, and both Muslims and non-Muslims alike worldwide are threatened by the imposition of Sharia. Until America is willing to have the courage to say that out loud, how can we stand against it? As a Christian, I will boldly call out and stand against any radical group claiming to share my faith while openly expressing hate and violence toward others. Many in the Muslim community have had the courage to do the same, like Aziz, who stood up and fought for what is right.

Unfortunately, the US government refuses to study the doctrine of Sharia or investigate the networks that propagate it worldwide (including in the United States), such as the Muslim Brotherhood. Organizations working with the Muslim Brotherhood are in part responsible for the push toward political correctness and a purging of factual information about Sharia in the military, federal law enforcement, and intelligence communities.

When you refuse to study your enemies' belief system, you can't name the actual problem. If you can't and won't name it, you won't know how best to fight it. This is how we lose the war on terror. We need to learn from the mistakes of our past and prepare ourselves now for the Taliban of the future, because they certainly will not look to coexist with America and the rest of the world. And, unfortunately, they now possess tens of billions of dollars' worth of our weapons and equipment. Worse yet, the same Muslim Brotherhood networks that influenced American foreign policy to be willfully blind to Sharia are still intact and as strong and influential as ever in American politics.

The Mission Continues

A few months after I returned from Tajikistan, Kathy accompanied me when I spoke at a Sunday morning church service in Washington, DC. Afterward, we met with five Afghan families who came to talk with us.

One family shared how they had left Kabul on one of our flights.

"Thank you," they said through tears.

A woman told me she had tried to contact me for two months. Her father had been targeted by the Taliban and killed. Other members of her family were still in the country even though they had all the needed paperwork to leave.

"Can you help them?" she asked, nearly collapsing in tears as her husband and Kathy held her upright.

A man introduced himself as a former interpreter recently flown to the United States with other evacuees.

"I just want to go back to Afghanistan with you and help," he said.

His wife added, "I want to go as well, please!"

What do you say in response to each of those? I have found myself in enough of those meetings with Afghan evacuees to give the best answers I know.

"You're welcome, but it was a whole bunch of people who were working together to get you here."

"We'll do the best we can."

"That would be awesome."

"We won't stop fighting."

What we say, though, is only a temporary help. Our words are mere place-holders because, ultimately, when people are in need, they care most about what you will do, not what you say.

Whatever is going on politically in and around Afghanistan, as long as American citizens, interpreters, and vulnerable groups are there, Save Our Allies will continue to explore every option to rescue them. We will continue to petition the government to do the right thing and help in every way we can when allowed.

As long as one American or ally needs rescuing from Afghanistan, we will do what is right.

In mid-October we were part of a coalition of organizations able to fly the FIFA girls soccer team out of a remote airport in Mazar-e Sharif and into Qatar. Counting family members, that was a rescue of about one hundred people. Those young girls no longer have to worry about having their lives ruined by the Taliban. That was a battle we needed to win, and we did.

About a week later, we flew Abdul Wasi Sharifi and several MMA fighters to Abu Dhabi. Abdul arranged to have mats donated so he could resume training his athletes at the humanitarian center. Kids inside the camp became fascinated watching the fighters train, and Abdul started a program at the center for more than a hundred kids to keep them busy and engaged in a positive and healthy activity. I am so proud of Abdul's leadership there and cannot wait to train with him when his team makes it to America. Abdul dreams of one day working for UFC, and I helped him take the first step toward making that dream come true by introducing him to UFC matchmaker Mick Maynard. Even though Abdul got out, we had five hundred other athletes—including world-ranked females—we were keeping hidden until we could arrange for them to leave.

In December, we partnered with another NGO and evacuated fifty-five US citizens and lawful permanent residents and flew them directly to New York City. More than a dozen children were in that group. We later partnered to get another twenty-three out in January 2022.

Maryam and Zahra, the two preacher's daughters who were separated from their family and made their way to Pakistan alone, as of this writing, are finally moving from the safe house I have been hiding them in for four months to a staging area to fly them to Qatar. Kathy and I have applied for humanitarian parole on their behalf to allow their temporary entrance into the United States for an urgent humanitarian reason. We have connected the young ladies with their father, mother, and brother so they can talk with each other. The family, which had been evacuated to Holloman Air Force Base in New Mexico, moved to Houston near Kathy and me in anticipation of Maryam and Zahra being brought here. Although Maryam and Zahra remain at risk in Pakistan, we are praying and working every day to get them out of there safely. Kathy and I look forward to witnessing their family reunion and helping them start their new life here in America.

Along with Maryam and Zahra, we are moving two hundred girls into safe houses; they will fly out in the coming days to Albania, Qatar, and Greece—doctors, journalists, teachers, athletes, and orphaned teenagers identified by the Taliban as targets to become war brides or to be killed. We also are working to rescue eight hundred Afghans in hiding who are immediate family members of seventy-six active-duty US service members.

On July 18, 2022, the State Department announced they have 74,274 principal SIV applicants and with an average family of 4.5, that is more than 334,233 pending applicants for SIV status living under Taliban rule. Others still have not been moved from humanitarian centers like Abu Dhabi. They are processing these on an average of 200 cases a week. A rate that will take 140 years to complete. Meanwhile our interpreters are being captured, persecuted, and executed by the Taliban for their service to America and stand against terrorism. The atrocities done to women and children and those who don't conform to Taliban ideology increase daily and the Doha Agreement (the "Taliban Peace Deal") prohibiting terrorism in Afghanistan has not been adhered to in the slightest, making Afghanistan a safe haven for terrorist like Al Qaeda.

What should we expect? Let's not forget the Taliban themselves are still a terrorist organization. There is no way for me to put a period on the end of a sentence that would conclude this story. The story and the work continues. It must.

Save Our Allies has evacuated more than seventeen thousand people. Although we've received widespread accolades, we're just one of a large group of NGOs, organizations, and people compelled to do the right thing and to take action. It has been exciting to see the positive responses and support for what everyone accomplished—all of us, not just Save Our Allies. Veterans' groups everywhere contributed to the effort. Partners like Mercury One, The Nazarene Fund, Task Force Argo, and Samaritan's Purse made flights possible. Groups like Task Force Pineapple, All Things Possible, Allied Airlift 2021, and of course my friend Dave Eubank and Free Burma Rangers were able to do great work from the United States, coordinating with the troops and allies on the ground to efficiently help thousands of people get into the gates and to safety. So many large and small endeavors were everywhere. I know I'm leaving out so many. Some managed to help hundreds or thousands of people—others, one or two people. All efforts were welcome and appreciated. We all did the best we could with what we had available.

Every active and former military member I've worked and talked with who's had any connection to rescuing people out of Afghanistan—and these are people whose combined total of military operations number well into the thousands—has been unanimous in declaring this effort the single most significant work in which they've ever participated in their lives. Our military missions were important, including our combat deployments. This, however, has been our most important work because it has been so tangible in its direct impact on human life.

But while we celebrate every single person who has found freedom again outside of Afghanistan, we cannot forget the remaining forty million people, including the twenty million women and girls, living in a nation that has been handed over to the evilest people in the world.

Because of them, we cannot claim victory. There is no victory in all of this. There is only doing the best we can do as the mission continues.

Conclusion

———— ★ ————

I TURNED ONTO MY STREET AND LOOKED TOWARD MY house. I'd driven into my driveway countless times after flying home. As much as I enjoyed coming home to my family each time, this time was different. My anticipation was like what a kid feels on Christmas morning as he heads for the tree.

Aziz was here, in my home.

He and his family were finally in their new country, the United States of America.

As I pulled into the driveway, I spotted Mashkorallah running joyfully across my front lawn, chasing my Vizsla, Daisy. It's such a familiar scene—a seven-year-old boy playing outside with a dog. But the moment got to me.

It had been more than eight months since we saved Aziz and his family. I'd created a position for Aziz at Mighty Oaks Foundation as our cultural advisor, planning to make use of his leadership abilities and experience to help guide our international work with interpreters and other countries' militaries. Two local churches had donated money and other resources and services to help his family transition into their new home and culture.

But the exuberance over getting them safely out of Afghanistan had eroded into fear they might not make it to the US. Aziz and his family had gotten stuck in the Abu Dhabi humanitarian center.

There had been more SIV paperwork nightmares. More problems because of that missing contract number. More US government confusion and inefficiency. More, presumably, slow walking by the State Department to avoid creating room for Save Our Allies and other NGOs to go get more Afghans and bring them to the UAE. At one point Aziz's family had been assigned a flight to the US, and then a measles outbreak among the evacuees halted those plans. Later his name was mysteriously pulled off a list, making him a no-go for America. When we addressed this with the US State Department, his removal was deemed a mistake. They apologized to Aziz and placed him back on the list.

In addition, protests by Afghan evacuees fed up with delays essentially forced a lockdown at the humanitarian center. Although it was far better than remaining in Afghanistan, the Afghans' temporary home became like a jail to them. They were free, but this wasn't the freedom they needed or were promised.

A worker from Mercury One noticed how exhausted Aziz's children were. "They need to get out of here," he told Aziz. "They need access to a normal life." He suggested Aziz apply for visas to Brazil.

Frustrated, I was tempted to tell Aziz to go to Brazil and we'd find a shortcut to get him to the US. I didn't want to do that. It wasn't the right way to bring the family here, but I'd pulled every string I had, and nothing was happening. I also worked on a plan to get the family to Qatar, but there was no guarantee I could bring them to the US from there.

Then I heard from my Kiwi friend "Mac," a member of the New Zealand elite Special Air Service. Mac worked with the manifests for flights out of the UAE, and we'd been talking regularly about Aziz's family's status.

"Hold off," Mac told me. "I think we're going to make it happen."

It did.

On Thursday, April 14, 2022, Aziz and his family boarded a flight for the US. Later that day they arrived in Virginia to begin two weeks of processing. This would plug them into the system so they could receive immigrants' benefits, limited as those are.

At the time Aziz flew to the US, I was in Ukraine with Seaspray, Dennis, and my son Hunter. After Russia invaded Ukraine, I knew our team's success in Afghanistan positioned us to assist evacuation efforts. We also learned of the severe need for medical supplies and support, so our team sprang into action.

At the request of Ukrainian military leaders, we took our Mighty Oaks spiritual resiliency programs to troops on the front lines. To the Ukrainians, the defense of their country represented a battle of good versus evil. Some of the leaders recognized the battle as spiritual, and they wanted to ensure their troops could maintain mental and spiritual resiliency throughout the war, a strategy that was working for them. Mighty Oaks' international division would now be composed of Dennis, Hunter, and Aziz. Who better to step up to the challenge?

Aziz's family flew to Houston after completing processing, and we set them up in an Airbnb near my home where they waited for me to return for our second long-awaited reunion.

To catch my flight for that homecoming, though, I had an extremely tight timeline to drive from Kyiv into Poland. Because of our operations in Ukraine, I hadn't showered in seven days. If you've never had the displeasure of that experience, then I will say that when you go a week without showering, you smell pretty sour. While I had sympathy for the other passengers on my flight since I wouldn't have time for a shower, I was determined to get home and see Aziz. But when I got into Poland, I miraculously had time to grab a quick shower and scrape off the sour smell.

On Thursday, May 5, I finally flew into Houston and headed toward home, thinking about the two reunions with Aziz. The first at the humanitarian center, where for the first time since the US troops' withdrawal I knew that Aziz and his family were safe. This time I knew Aziz was safe, but the experience felt just as surreal as the day I knocked on his door in Abu Dhabi.

Kathy was the first to greet me as I walked up the sidewalk. Mashkorallah and Daisy were next, followed by the two older boys. Then Aziz came over and latched onto me with that big ol' bear hug of his.

Then Kahtera stepped toward me.

At the reunion in Abu Dhabi, Aziz's wife had remained at the back of the room in line with Afghan custom, and we'd greeted each other from a distance by placing our hands over our hearts. But this time, for the first time, Kahtera and I embraced with a hug.

"Thank you, brother," she told me. Kahtera already seemed comfortable in her new home. In her new culture.

While Aziz and his family were in Virginia and I was in Ukraine, we had a conversation in which we reflected on how a mission to save Aziz had turned into rescuing seventeen thousand Afghans. We relived the six years of anguish and prayer working to obtain his SIV. The delays had seemed so needless back then.

"Maybe God didn't allow it to happen because it wasn't His timing," Aziz said. "I still had to be there when the US withdrew because God knew that you would come to get me, and that would result in a great rescue of all those other people."

Acknowledgments

———— ★ ————

WE WILL ALL HAVE VARIOUS SEASONS OF LIFE. WE WILL have highs and lows, finding ourselves in dark valleys some days and on high mountaintops other days. There will be times in life when you will be in dire need of help and other times when you will be in the position to help someone else. When you find yourself there and you alone have the ability to help, you must! We were created to. It is who we are by design.

> Greater love has no one than this, that someone lay down his life for his friends. (John 15:13 ESV)

Regardless of religion, race, nationality, or political affiliation, we are all part of the same human race. We are interconnected. So if we have the ability to help someone else, we must. If we have the opportunity to do the right thing for someone in a critical time of need, we must. We were created to.

It was extremely humbling to see those from all different faiths and walks of life come together to help when the governments of the world wouldn't.

Thank you, God, for the blessing of burdening our hearts with a response to those in need, and then orchestrating what it takes to meet those needs.

Thank you to the initial twelve members of our team who said yes to taking action when others wouldn't. Thank you to the organizations and volunteers who united from around the world when tears and cries for help came

Acknowledgments

from Afghanistan. Our actions demonstrated that humanity and unity still exist in this broken world.

Thank you all for the love, prayers, and support from thousands across the globe who got behind us to accomplish this mission. Because of each of you, Aziz and his family and over seventeen thousand others can live free of death and persecution.

Last and never least, I would like to thank my family and the entire Mighty Oaks Foundation staff for always being supportive of me and the burdens God lays on my heart. You all continue to give me the support and bandwidth to do the things God calls me to do.

The mission continues.

Notes

─────── ★ ───────

Foreword by Glenn Beck

1. Winston Churchill, "We Shall Fight on the Beaches," speech, House of Commons, June 4, 1940, https://winstonchurchill.org/resources/speeches /1940-the-finest-hour/we-shall-fight-on-the-beaches/.
2. Churchill, "We Shall Fight on the Beaches."

Chapter 4: Poor Processes and Bad Decisions

1. Ailsa Chang, Casey Morell, and Amy Isackson, "U.S. Special Immigrant Visa Program Faces Criticism Over Slow Speed," NPR, August 16, 2021, https:// www.npr.org/2021/08/16/1028198510/u-s-special-immigrant-visa-program -faces-criticism-over-slow-speed.
2. Mark Meadows, *The Chief's Chief* (St. Petersburg, FL: All Seasons Press, 2021), 284–85.
3. Joseph Choi, "US Left Bagram Airfield at Night, Didn't Inform Afghan Commander: Report," MSN, July 6, 2021, https://www.msn.com/en-us/news /world/us-left-bagram-airfield-at-night-didnt-inform-afghan-commander -report/ar-AALPtwA.
4. "Press Briefing by Press Secretary Jen Psaki, July 8, 2021," The White House, July 8, 2021, https://www.whitehouse.gov/briefing-room/press-briefings /2021/07/08/press-briefing-by-press-secretary-jen-psaki-july-8-2021/.
5. Bob Fredericks, "US Says Nearly 800 ISIS Members on Ground When 'Mother of All Bombs' Dropped," *New York Post*, April 13, 2007, https://nypost.com /2017/04/13/us-says-nearly-800-isis-members-on-ground-when-mother-of-all -bombs-dropped/.

6. See "Afghanistan Fatalities," Iraq Coalition Casualty Count, accessed January 7, 2022, http://www.icasualties.org/App/AfghanFatalities.

7. "Trump Plans to Slash U.S. Troop Numbers in Germany," Statista, June 8, 2020, https://www.statista.com/chart/17355/us-military-overseas/.

Chapter 5: Who Surrendered to the Taliban?

1. Jerry Dunleavy, "Milley May Have Undercounted Number of Afghan Forces Who Died in War with Taliban," MSN, September 1, 2021, https://www.msn .com/en-us/news/world/milley-may-have-undercounted-number-of-afghan -forces-who-died-in-war-with-taliban/ar-AANZNUJ.

2. *Left Behind: A Brief Assessment of the Biden Administration's Strategic Failures During the Afghanistan Evacuation*, United States Senate Committee on Foreign Relations Minority Report (redacted), February 2022, PDF, https://www .foreign.senate.gov/imo/media/doc/Risch%20Afghanistan%20Report %202022.pdf.

3. *Left Behind*, 53.

4. Yaroslav Trofimov, Dion Nissenbaum, and Margherita Stancati, "'Saigon on Steroids': The Desperate Rush to Flee Afghanistan," *Wall Street Journal*, August 15, 2021, https://www.wsj.com/articles/saigon-on-steroids-the-desperate -rush-to-flee-afghanistan-11629071999.

5. Eric Lutz, "As Afghanistan Unravels, Biden's Foreign Policy Agenda Faces Its First Real Test," *Vanity Fair*, August 13, 2021, https://www.vanityfair.com /news/2021/08/as-afghanistan-unravels-biden-foreign-policy-agenda-faces -first-real-test.

Chapter 7: Chaos at the Airport

1. Myah Ward, "Biden Says U.S. Will Stay in Afghanistan until All Americans Who Want to Leave Can Do So," Politico, August 18, 2021, https://www .politico.com/news/2021/08/18/biden-says-us-will-stay-in-afghanistan-until -all-americans-allies-who-want-to-leave-can-do-so-506112.

2. Mark Landler and Megan Stack, "Taliban Reject Extended Deadline as U.S. Races to Finish Evacuation," *New York Times*, August 23, 2021, https://www .nytimes.com/2021/08/23/world/asia/afghanistan-evacuation-americans-biden .html.

3. US Congress, Congressional Record, Senate, vol. 167, no. 164 (September 22, 2021), https://www.congress.gov/congressional-record/2021/9/22/senate-section /article/s6609-1.

Chapter 11: Leaving Afghanistan

1. Barbara Sprunt, "Biden Pledges to Strike Back After Attack Kills 13 U.S. Service Members in Kabul," NPR, August 26, 2021, https://www.npr .org/2021/08/26/1031330557/biden-remarks-troops-killed-kabul-afghanistan.

2. "Military Officials Brief Media on Investigation Results of ISIS-K Bombing at Abbey Gate," US Central Command, press release, February 4, 2022, https:// www.centcom.mil/MEDIA/PRESS-RELEASES/Press-Release-View /Article/2923951/military-officials-brief-media-on-investigation-results-of -isis-k-bombing-at-ab/; Jeremy Her, et al., "Pentagon Says Deadly Afghan Airport Attack Was Carried Out by a Single Suicide Bomber and Not a Complex Operation," CNN, updated February 4, 2022, https://www.cnn .com/2022/02/04/politics/pentagon-kabul-airport-investigation/index.html.

Chapter 12: Unfinished Business

1. Christine Goldbaun, "Facing Economic Collapse, Afghanistan Is Gripped by Starvation," *New York Times*, December 4, 2021, https://www.nytimes .com/2021/12/04/world/asia/afghanistan-starvation-crisis.html.

Chapter 18: Heartbreak Among Success

1. "Ahmad Massoud: 'I Would Prefer to Die Than to Surrender,'" SAMAA, August 26, 2021, https://www.samaaenglish.tv/news/2399234.

Chapter 19: The Journey Ahead

1. For more on the Wakhan Corridor, see Sam Dunning, "China Is Protecting Its Thin Corridor to the Afghan Heartland," *Foreign Policy*, August 14, 2021, https://foreignpolicy.com/2021/08/14/china-afghanistan-wakhan-corridor -imperial-ambitions/.

2. Andrew Mark Miller and Lucas Y. Tomlinson, "More Military Service Members Committed Suicide July–Sept 21 Than Have Ever Died from Coronavirus," Fox News, January 8, 2022, https://www.foxnews.com/politics /nearly-twice-military-members-died-suicide-coronavirus-since-pandemic-start.

3. *Supporting Afghanistan Allies*, Pulse Check, Blue Star Families, September 2021, https://bluestarfam.org/research/.

About the Author

━━━━━ ★ ━━━━━

CHAD ROBICHAUX IS A FORMER FORCE RECON MARINE AND DoD contractor, with eight deployments to Afghanistan as part of a ███ Special Operations ███ Task Force. After overcoming his personal battles with PTSD and nearly becoming a veteran suicide statistic, Chad founded the Mighty Oaks Foundation. This leading nonprofit serves the active duty, military veteran, and first responder communities with highly successful, faith-based combat trauma and resiliency programs. Chad has become a go-to resource and is considered a subject-matter expert on faith-based solutions to PTSD. He's spoken to more than 400,000 active-duty troops, led lifesaving programs for more than 4,500 active military and veterans at five Mighty Oaks ranches, was appointed to serve as the chairman of a White House veterans coalition, and advised a former presidential administration, Congress, the VA, and the DoD.

He is also the cofounder of Save Our Allies, a nonprofit mission focused on the evacuation and recovery of Americans, US allies, and vulnerable people trapped in Afghanistan. Save Our Allies began as a personal quest for Chad, as he set out to rescue his longtime friend and interpreter, but the mission quickly evolved because of Chad's compassion for people and his servant heart. Since its inception, Save Our Allies has safely evacuated more than seventeen thousand people who were trapped in Afghanistan, and the organization is now helping in Ukraine.

Chad is a bestselling author and has written a number of books related to veteran care and overcoming life's challenges, donating more than 250,000 copies to the troops during his resiliency speaking tours. He is regularly featured on national media outlets, and his story was notably shared in a short film by *I Am Second* and the documentary *Never Fight Alone*.

In addition to Chad's military career, he has served our nation as both a special agent with the US Federal Air Marshal Service and a surveillance detection senior program manager with the US State Department. Chad is a Medal of Valor recipient for his bravery beyond the call of duty in law enforcement. He earned an MBA from New York Institute of Technology and is a board-certified pastoral counselor with a focus on PTSD. Chad is married to his wife of twenty-seven years, Kathy, and they have a daughter, two sons, and two granddaughters. His sons, Hunter and Hayden, are both third-generation Marines in the Robichaux family and share Chad's passion for martial arts. Chad is also a fourth-degree Brazilian Jiu-Jitsu black belt under the legendary Master Carlson Gracie Jr. and a former professional mixed martial arts champion.